# CONSTRUCTION ADJUDICATION

# CONSTRUCTION ADJUDICATION

Robert Stevenson
*Solicitor, Berrymans Lace Mawer, London*

and

Peter Chapman
*Chartered Civil Engineer and Barrister, 46 Essex Street, London*

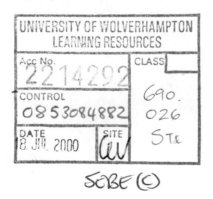

JORDANS
1999

Published by
Jordan Publishing Limited
21 St Thomas Street
Bristol BS1 6JS

**British Library Cataloguing-in-Publication Data**
A catalogue record for this book is available from the British Library.


ISBN 0 85308 488 2


Typeset by Mendip Communications Ltd, Frome, Somerset
Printed by MPG Books Ltd, Bodmin, Cornwall

# Foreword

At the time of writing this foreword, the Housing Grants, Construction and Regeneration Act 1996 has been in force for a year. There is as yet little sign of a flood of requests for adjudicators to be appointed.

It may be, of course, that disputing parties are harmoniously agreeing on the identity of their adjudicators but, even allowing for this, the number of adjudications taking place seems to be relatively small. There could be many different reasons for this, and a programme of research will be required before we can gain such understanding.

Whatever the propensity to make use of the new right to adjudication, it is worth commenting that the number of adjudications held will not be a good measure of the success of this Act.

If the Act is to have a real impact, as I hope and believe it will, that impact will lie in the adjudications which do *not* take place. It will lie in the changed behaviour of parties who reconcile their differences because they know that an adjudicator can be called in at any time to apply an impartial view to the issue, and to give a decision. Since its publication in 1993, the New Engineering Contract has given this opporunity for immediate adjudication of disputes, but for those operating under most other forms of contract this is a huge practical and psychological change.

So too is the concept of a right to leave site for want of due payment. It will be some years before we can know how the construction industry and the various related professions have adapted to these two new circumstances.

Meanwhile one assertion can be confidently made. Whether for matters relating to payment, for the purpose of pursuing or defending an adjudication, or for the wisdom of reaching a conclusion without one, it is important that all practitioners in the construction industry fully understand the Act. Whatever the eventual patterns of behaviour, one thing is certain: from 1 May 1998, the rules of the game are different. All players need to know and understand the new rules.

This is what makes this volume by Robert Stevenson and Peter Chapman so valuable. It not only brings together all the relevant documentation on the Act and the Scheme, but it provides a commentary at two levels: what the Act says, and how to apply it. It is a true guide to this piece of legislation and I commend it to all those with a role in construction.

ROGER SAINSBURY
*President*
*Institution of Civil Engineers*
*August 1999*

# Preface

The Housing Grants, Construction and Regeneration Act 1996 came into force in 1998. With the passage of time, an increasing number of construction contracts are now subject to its provision and 1999 has seen an increasing number of adjudications being initiated. Enforcement of a number of decisions has been necessary and the Technology and Construction Court has ruled on a number of occasions, discussion of these judgments is included in this book.

We have also drawn on our experience as adjudicators and advisers to parties in litigation as well as the experience of colleagues and friends in this new departure in dispute resolution for the UK construction industry. We extend our thanks to them, but especially to Pauline Bowman and Wendy Warmington who have worked so hard to put our thoughts into some semblance of order, and also to Anke, Vanessa and Tania for their help in research.

ROBERT STEVENSON
AND
PETER CHAPMAN
*October 1999*

# Acknowledgements

The authors and publishers gratefully acknowledge the kind permission of the following organisations to reproduce the following materials in Appendix 3.

The Technology and Construction Solicitors Association in respect of the 1999 Version 1.3 of its Procedural Rules for Adjudication (at p 131).

The Institution of Civil Engineers in respect of the Adjudication Procedure 1997, published by Thomas Telford Limited, London, 1997 (at p 137).

The Construction Industry Council in respect of its Model Adjudication Procedure: Second Edition (at p 145).

The Centre for Dispute Resolution in respect of its Rules for Adjudication, Application for Appointment of Adjudicator and Adjudication Agreement (at p 153).

Fédération Internationale des Ingénieurs-Conseils in respect of the Supplement to the Fourth Edition 1987 of Conditions of Contract for Works of Civil Engineering Construction: Section A – Dispute Adjudication Board; Model Terms of Appointment; and Procedural Rules (at p 165).

# Biographical details

**Robert Stevenson FCIArb**

Robert Stevenson is a Solicitor and Partner in the Construction Engineering Group of Berrymans Lace Mawer in London. He has practised in the field of construction law for over 15 years, in the UK, France and in the Far East. He is an accredited TeCSA Adjudicator.

**Peter H J Chapman BSc LLB FICE FCIArb FconsE FHKIE FIHT**

Peter Chapman is a Chartered Civil Engineer, Chartered Arbitrator and Barrister-at-Law. He has, for the last ten years, acted principally as arbitrator, adjudicator and mediator/conciliator in engineering and construction disputes. Throughout his career, he has been associated with major projects such as the mass transit railway systems in London, Hong Kong and Singapore, hydroelectric and thermal power projects in Europe, Asia and Africa and large bridges, roads and airports in various parts of the Far East. He has served on eight dispute boards, acting as chairman on several occasions. He has acted as adjudicator in well over 100 construction disputes. He has Chambers at 46 Essex Street, London WC2R 3GH.

# Contents

# Table of Cases

References are to paragraph numbers; *italic* page numbers are to Appendix material.

# Table of Statutes

References are to paragraph numbers; *italic* page numbers are to Appendix material; **bold italic** page numbers show *where material is set out*.

# Table of Statutory Instruments

References are to paragraph numbers; *italic* page numbers are to Appendix material; **bold italic** page numbers show where material is set out.

# Table of Rules, Conditions and Contracts etc

References are to paragraph numbers; *italic* page numbers are to Appendix material; ***bold italic*** page numbers show where material is set out.

# Table of Conventions

References are to paragraph numbers.

# Table of Abbreviations

| | |
|---|---|
| 1996 Act | Housing Grants, Construction and Regeneration Act 1996 |
| 1999 Act | Contract (Rights of Third Parties) Act 1999 |
| ACE | Association of Consulting Engineers |
| ADR | alternative dispute resolution |
| BEC | Building Employers Confederation |
| BPF | British Property Federation |
| CEDR | Centre for Dispute Resolution |
| CIArb | Chartered Institute of Arbitrators |
| CIC | Construction Industry Council |
| CoWa/F | Collateral Warranty (France) |
| CPR 1998 | Civil Procedure Rules 1998 |
| DRB | dispute review board |
| FIDIC | Fédération Internationale des Ingénieurs-Conseils |
| ICE | Institution of Civil Engineers |
| JCT | Joint Contracts Tribunal |
| JCT 80 | Joint Contracts Tribunal Standard Form of Building Contract 1980 Edition |
| MCWa/F | Main Contractor Warranty (Funder) |
| NEC | New Engineering Contract |
| OR | Official Referee |
| ORBA | Official Referees Bar Association |
| ORSA | Official Referees' Solicitors' Association (now TeCSA) |
| PFI | private finance initiative |
| RIBA | Royal Institute of British Architects |
| RICS | Royal Institution of Chartered Surveyors |
| The Scheme | Scheme for Construction Contracts |
| SCOSS | Standing Committee for Structural Safety |
| TCC | Technology Construction Court |
| TECBAR | Technology and Construction Court Barristers' Association |
| TeCSA | Technology and Construction Solicitors Association |

# Chapter 1

## INTRODUCTION

### 1.1 WHAT IS ADJUDICATION?

This book is, in large measure, prompted by the inclusion in the Housing Grants, Construction and Regeneration Act 1996 (the 1996 Act) of the requirement that all construction contracts shall henceforth contain an 'adjudication clause'.

The 1996 Act itself does not define 'adjudication'; it simply sets out a number of requirements which an adjudication clause has to meet in order to comply with the Act.

To adjudicate, in its widest sense, means to hear and settle a case by judicial procedure. The word often occurs in such areas as mental health reviews and even in decisions of the court. In the construction industry, it has come to refer to a particular method of resolving disputes. An independent party or tribunal appointed under the contract renders a decision which is then binding for a period of time, or until it is reviewed by another tribunal, which may be an arbitrator, or the courts.

The mere fact that a clause in a contract is called an 'adjudication clause' does not necessarily mean that it satisfies the requirements of the 1996 Act. Upon examination of the clause, a court may decide that what the parties in fact intended was arbitration. An arbitration leads, of course, to a final and binding decision.[1]

### 1.2 ADJUDICATION IN UK CONSTRUCTION CONTRACTS PRIOR TO THE HOUSING GRANTS, CONSTRUCTION AND REGENERATION ACT 1996

Adjudication clauses have been included in standard form English construction sub-contracts for approximately 35 years. Most developers and their advisers use one of the various forms published by the Joint Contracts Tribunal (JCT). The predecessor to the current JCT sub-contracts (the green form), a standard form of nominated sub-contract, dates from 1963. The blue form, for non-nominated domestic sub-contractors, dates from 1971. Both contained adjudication clauses which enabled a sub-contractor to challenge, within strict time-limits, amounts payable to the sub-contractor which the contractor had set-off or deducted from an interim payment.

---

1    *Cape Durasteel Ltd, Rosser and Russell Building Services* (1996) 46 Con LR 75.

The JCT draws its membership from all sides of the construction industry. The green and blue forms referred to above were approved for use by the Building Employers Confederation (BEC) (formerly the NFBTE), the Federation of Associations of Specialists and Sub-Contractors, and the Committee of Associations of Specialist Engineering Contractors. The JCT 1980 Edition of the Domestic Sub-Contract Conditions (DOM/1), the JCT Nominated Sub-Contract Conditions (NSC/C) and the NAM/SC sub-contract form for use with the JCT Intermediate Form of Sub-Contract (IFC 84) all provided for the sub-contractor to challenge what he considered to be an unjustified set-off from sums otherwise due by referring the dispute to an adjudicator who was named in the contract. If no one had been named, or the named individual was incapable of acting, an adjudicator would be appointed by the BEC.

Once the adjudicator was in a position to act, the contract laid down the timetable for submissions by the parties. The adjudicator's decision was limited to whether or not he determined that the main contractor's set-off was justified either in whole or in part. If he considered that it was unjustified, he would order payment to be made to the sub-contractor; alternatively, he could also order the sums in dispute to be deposited with a stakeholder. The adjudicator's decision was stated to be binding until the dispute had been settled by agreement or determined by an arbitrator or the court.

The important features of the provisions relating to set-off were as follows:

(1)  they were limited to disputes over main contractors exercising set-off against sums otherwise due to the sub-contractor, and were not concerned with other issues such as valuation;
(2)  the adjudicator's decision was stated to be binding until the matter was finally agreed or settled by the court or arbitration. Indeed, there was a requirement on the sub-contractor to serve notice of arbitration *at the same time as* sending his notice of objection to the contractor and requesting adjudication;
(3)  they differed markedly from the requirements for adjudication introduced by ss 104–117 of the 1996 Act.

The operation of these albeit limited adjudication clauses resulted in two cases of note, *Cameron v John Mowlem & Co plc*[1] and *Drake & Scull Engineering Ltd v McLaughlin & Harvey plc*,[2] which will be examined in later chapters.

Apart from the standard form contracts referred to above, since the mid-1980s adjudication provisions have been introduced into bespoke construction contracts for UK projects such as fixed link crossings, railway works (capital expenditure and maintenance) and highway construction. These special applications emerged from two sources: first, due to the success and economy of expert determination dispute-resolution provisions commonly utilised in property valuation disputes and commodity contract disputes; and, secondly, due to the growth in popularity

---

1    (1990) 52 BLR 24.
2    (1995) 60 BLR 102.

of construction industry dispute review boards in the USA and other parts of the world.

Adjudication by single adjudicators or tribunals of three or more was established by contract, usually at the commencement of the project, and provided for recommendations (or decisions) on matters where the contracting parties were unable to agree. The adjudicators were encouraged to take a proactive approach, to adopt inquisitorial procedures and to dispense with much of the usual 'litigation' routines in order to reach speedy conclusions. The aim was for adjudicators, who were persons experienced both in the technical aspects of the project and in construction dispute-resolution, to devise common sense and fair solutions to the disputes.

Solutions were to be faithful to contractual provisions and, in the many instances where the contract was non-absolute in its intent, acceptable to both parties, thereby avoiding arbitration. The adjudication process was therefore essentially 'judicial', while also relying on the specialist knowledge and experience of the adjudicator or tribunal. A distinctive feature in many of these bespoke adjudication arrangements was the necessity for the adjudicator or tribunal to take a close and active interest in the project throughout construction, not merely to become involved when the dispute arose. This aspect is discussed in more detail in Chapter 6.

The contractual provisions under which the adjudication process was established and procedures were specified varied considerably, as did the manner of composition of the larger tribunals. In most cases, the contracts stated time periods within which the dispute had to be brought to adjudication, and the recommendation or decision had to be made. Such provisions were drafted before the coming into force of the 1996 Act and, consequently, are different from the statutory arrangements now in force.

Several projects which have involved adjudication arrangements (many of which are under construction at the time of publication) are private finance initiative (PFI) schemes and are therefore exempt from the provisions of the 1996 Act. Further, under such contracts, the financial arrangements (both during construction and during the operation of any related concession) may be complex and, in anticipation of financial disputes, contracts may provide for additional tribunals to deal solely with financial disputes.

## 1.3 ADJUDICATION IN INTERNATIONAL CONSTRUCTION PROJECTS

Projects which involve the skills and resources of main contractors and consultants, who are domiciled outside the country where the construction is taking place, are referred to as 'international' projects. The majority of civil engineering works undertaken in Third World countries (where construction contracting is still developing) is thus classified as international. It is common for such projects to be funded by loans from international banking organisations such as the World Bank, the European Bank for Reconstruction and Development, the Asian Development Bank and the African Development Bank.

International projects generally involve infrastructural construction work – the building of roads, railways, dams, power stations and airports. Much of the work is undertaken in undeveloped and often inaccessible regions where there is a greater risk of political, economic and technical problems, leading to contractual claims involving considerable amounts of money. In international projects, because of the relative inexperience of the project owner (usually a State enterprise) and the heavy borrowings which are necessary to undertake the project, the resolution of claims using the internal contractual mechanisms (eg the engineer in his quasi-judicial capacity or by party negotiation) will fail to produce satisfactory settlements.

An international contractor may, therefore, have to commence arbitration proceedings, possibly in Paris or Stockholm under International Chamber of Commerce or other recognised rules, to enforce his contractual rights. Under the provisions of most contracts, arbitration is precluded until the works have been completed but as the arbitral process involves a reconstruction of past events for the benefit of the tribunal by the time the arbitral proceedings take place, the persons who best know the facts in dispute are often unavailable to testify as they have moved on elsewhere.

The time and costs involved in international arbitration (and the nature of the remedies finally obtained) have led to an understandable reluctance to pursue this course. Tender prices (and, consequently, construction costs) have reflected this uncertainty in dispute-resolution.

A more expeditious and practical method of dispute-resolution for international projects was required to provide satisfactory solutions to the parties' differences during the duration of the construction and to produce 'real-time' benefits which would assist the performance of the contract. Drawing from the experiences in the USA, where adjudication by disputes review boards (DRBs) had achieved considerable success, dispute boards have now been established for numerous international projects. These boards, usually comprising three independent construction professionals experienced in both technical and contractual matters, become conversant with the project by undertaking routine visits to site and reading progress reports. In the event that a dispute arises which cannot be settled by the parties, the DRB is called upon to adjudicate the matter. The decision of the DRB may be entirely non-binding, or binding unless arbitration is commenced within a specified time, depending on the terms of the contract. However, even non-binding decisions (in effect, recommendations) are recognised as being highly persuasive before any subsequent arbitrator or the courts.

The success of the early DRBs on international projects encouraged the World Bank (in 1995) and, more recently, the Fédération Internationale des Ingénieurs-Conseils (FIDIC) to promote their use in projects of significant financial value. Standard provisions have been drafted for the set-up and operation of DRBs. Furthermore, both the World Bank and FIDIC have provided in their own standard documents for one-man boards to adjudicate over projects of more modest value.

DRBs are now employed throughout the world – especially in the USA, the UK, China, South Africa, India, Pakistan, Sweden and Denmark – and have been used on some prestigious projects, including the Channel Tunnel, the Channel Tunnel Rail Link and the new Hong Kong International Airport. There are also several large projects nearing completion (notably in China, Lesotho and the UK) in which all current contractual disputes have been settled with the assistance of the DRB. See Chapter 6 for a more detailed discussion of DRBs.

## 1.4 THE GROWTH OF ADJUDICATION CLAUSES

Adjudication provisions were originally introduced in standard form sub-contracts to prevent interim payments to sub-contractors being reduced or eliminated altogether by the main contractor by arguments of set-off. Litigation or arbitration over set-off often involved a lengthy examination of the issues and, in the meantime, the sub-contractor was starved of cash flow – 'the life blood of the enterprise'.[1] However, the procedure was limited and could be circumvented. The adjudicator's jurisdiction was restricted to a consideration of the validity of the main contractor's set-off; he could not, for example, consider the value of the sub-contract works. This restriction meant that a main contractor could argue before the court that the reason for non-payment was because of a dispute over the value of the sub-contract works.

Another reason for the growth in adjudication clauses was the reduced role of the contract administrator (whether architect or engineer), named in the contract between employer and contractor and acting in a quasi-judicial capacity when reviewing the claims of the parties (usually those of the contractor).

In the UK the most widely used form of civil engineering contract is produced by the Institution of Civil Engineers (ICE). Before the implementation of the 1996 Act, this form provided that any dispute between the employer and the contractor had to be referred in the first instance to the engineer appointed under the contract, whose decision remained binding until either a recommendation by a conciliator is accepted by the parties or revised by an arbitrator's award. Under the JCT Standard Form of Building Contract, 1980 Edition (JCT 80), an architect appointed as the contract administrator does not have such a clearly defined role of first review. Nevertheless, he exercises an important function in considering the contractor's applications for extensions of time and additional payment, and reviewing these applications within 12 weeks from the date fixed for completion. The architect can extend, shorten or confirm his earlier decisions on the date for completion of the contract. Contractors use this opportunity to review to submit more detailed submissions as to why they should be entitled to extensions of time and, by implication, payment for loss and expense.

---

1    Per Lord Denning in *Gilbert Ash (Northern) Limited v Modern Engineering (Bristol) Limited* [1974] AC 689.

In order that the procedure works effectively and that the decision is accepted by both parties, the contract administrator must appear impartial, and removed from the parties, which may be difficult to achieve in practice.

Frequently, the contract administrator is asked to revise his own earlier decision. The contractor may be seeking a further extension of time because of an alleged failure on the contract administrator's part to deliver design drawings on time. The contract supervisor in effect is being asked to concede that he himself has delayed the contract. Consequently, if an extension is granted on such grounds, the contract supervisor himself will be the subject of a claim from his employer.

Contractors have become sceptical about the true independence of the contract administrator. For their part, some employers have come to view their impartial reviewing role as incompatible with their duty to their client.

The use of DRBs, both nationally and internationally, and the provision of an adjudicator in the New Engineering Contract, 2nd Edition (ICE, 1995) (NEC) was, in part, a response to this.

Arbitration is still the most popular method of resolving disputes in building and engineering contracts. The use of arbitration was reinforced in *Northern Regional Health Authority v Derek Crouch Construction Ltd*[1] where it was held that only an arbitrator had the power to review or 'open up' the certificate of an architect or engineer. This meant that at least one party in a construction contract, where an engineer or an architect had such a certifying role, had an interest in requiring an arbitration clause. The decision was much criticised but remained the law for the majority of such contracts, until it was overruled in *Beaufort Developments (NI) Ltd v Gilbert Ash (NI) Ltd and Others.*[2] As a consequence, arbitrators no longer have more extensive powers than a judge, and parties can now choose between arbitration and court proceedings for resolving any disputes.

Arbitration has been seen increasingly as slow and as expensive as court proceedings, with the added disadvantage of the cost of employing the arbitrator and the potential challenge to his jurisdiction and eventual award. These perceptions may change. Lord Bingham, the Lord Chief Justice, has stated that the emphasis of the Arbitration Act 1996 is on providing 'a speedy and cost effective resolution of disputes by an impartial (probably expert often non-legal) tribunal in accordance with procedures very largely determined by the parties and with no, or at worst minimal, intervention by the courts'.[3]

## 1.5 THE LATHAM REPORT

In July 1993, the then Joint Under Secretary of State, Tony Baldry, announced a joint review of procurement and contractual arrangements in the UK construction industry. Unlike earlier reviews in the construction industry (such as the Banwell

---

1    [1984] QB 644.
2    [1998] 2 WLR 860, HL (NI).
3    Foreword to *The Arbitration Act 1996* (Blackwell Science in conjunction with the Chartered Institute of Arbitrators, 1996) by Bruce Harns, Rowan Planterose and Jonathan Tecks.

Report in 1984), government departments and construction bodies which funded and supported the review requested that it be carried out by a single reviewer and not a group working collectively. The reviewer was, however, to be assisted by six assessors drawing from the participating government department and construction industry bodies. Sir Michael Latham, a former Conservative Party MP, was appointed to produce a review within one year, with an interim report before Christmas 1993.

Sir Michael Latham produced interim and final reports, entitled, respectively, *Trust and Money* and *Constructing the Team* (July 1994).[1] The latter made 30 recommendations, some, but by no means all of which, required legislation. The recommendations included the outlawing of certain unfair contract clauses, the setting-up of mandatory trust funds for construction work, a change in the law of liability in construction contracts, a requirement for a decennial type of insurance for commercial and retail construction projects, and a requirement that adjudication 'should be the normal method of dispute resolution'.

This book is concerned only with adjudication and, to an extent, the outlawing of certain contract clauses concerning payment, which are dealt with in Chapter 5. The other legislative proposals of the Latham Report have yet to be enacted.

Sir Michael Latham was impressed by the NEC (now the New Engineering and Construction Contract), and considered that it was capable of becoming a common contract for the whole industry, although amendments and additions to its family of contracts were required. All disputes under the NEC arising during the course of the contract are referred to the decision of an adjudicator. The text of the Latham Report's recommendations on dispute-resolution are reproduced in Appendix 2.

## 1.6 THE HOUSING GRANTS, CONSTRUCTION AND REGENERATION ACT 1996

The 1996 Act embodies some of the recommendations contained in the Latham Report. The report recommended that a system of adjudication be included in all standard form contracts, underpinned by legislation. The report also recommended that:

(1) there should be no restrictions on the issues capable of being referred to the adjudicator, conciliator or mediator, either in the main contract or in sub-contracts;
(2) the award of the adjudicator should be implemented immediately. The use of stakeholders should be permitted only if both parties agree or if the adjudicator so directs;
(3) any appeal to arbitration or to the court should be after practical completion, and should not be allowed to delay the implementation of the award, unless an immediate and exceptional issue arises. The report also suggested that the

---

1    Published by HMSO.

courts may wish to support the system of adjudication by agreeing expedited procedures for interim payments.

In coming to these recommendations, Sir Michael Latham was assisted by a number of working parties representing the clients, consultants, main contractors and specialist and trade contractors. Sir Michael's hope was that other changes to procurement practices, contract conditions and the rights of set-off would lessen the recourse to arbitration in the courts, and adjudication would become the normal method of resolving disputes.

## 1.7   ALTERNATIVE METHODS OF DISPUTE-RESOLUTION

### 1.7.1   Arbitration

Alternative dispute-resolution (ADR) is broadly a method of resolving disputes other than in court. In this sense, arbitration is also a method of ADR which has been part of English commercial law for centuries. However, ADR is most commonly applied to non-binding dispute-resolution, such as conciliation and mediation. Growing dissatisfaction with the expense and inflexibility of arbitration procedures, coupled with a desire to clarify the law on arbitration, led to the Arbitration Act 1996.

The Act allows the parties a large measure of freedom in deciding their own procedures but, where they have not done so, it provides a framework in which arbitration can operate.

Section 1(b) of the Arbitration Act 1996 states that the parties should be free to agree how disputes are resolved, subject only to such safeguards as are necessary in the public interest. The Act has certain mandatory provisions, which include the immunity of arbitrators (s 29), the enforcement of awards (s 66) and the staying of legal proceedings where there is a valid arbitration clause (ss 9–11). Other provisions of the Act are non-mandatory, allowing the parties to make their own arrangements, but provide rules which apply in the absence of agreement. For example, if the parties do not specify the number of arbitrators, the tribunal shall consist of a sole arbitrator (s 15).

Arbitration awards, once delivered, can be enforced by a relatively simple procedure. Mutual recognition of arbitration awards internationally is now provided in many countries under the auspices of the New York Convention of 1958.

### 1.7.2   Non-binding forms of ADR

Alternative forms of dispute-resolution have risen in popularity in recent years, partly due to dissatisfaction over the cost and expense of court proceedings and/or arbitration. Such forms of ADR include mediation, conciliation, executive review and mini trials. All forms of ADR look to a settlement or agreement, rather than a decision imposed or ruled upon by a third party. Many contracts now permit the parties to submit their dispute to conciliation or mediation before they proceed to arbitration or litigation. For example, the ICE Conditions of Contract, Sixth Edition include this provision. In some contracts the parties must pass through this stage before proceeding to arbitration or litigation. However, whether it is optional or mandatory, no binding decision can be reached unless the parties agree to it.

### 1.7.3 Expert determination

Expert determination clauses have been used for many years in a wide variety of contracts, including commodity contracts, rent reviews, oil and gas industry agreements, and in the construction industry generally. Although they are sometimes confused with arbitration clauses, expert determination clauses are very different.

The typical wording of expert clauses, which emphasises the distinction, states that the person so nominated shall 'rule as an expert and not as an arbitrator'.

The principal reasons why these clauses are different from arbitration clauses are that:

(a) they are not arbitrations, they are not subject to the Arbitration Act 1996, and an expert decision, when rendered, may be binding depending on the terms of the contract establishing the procedure, but is not immediately enforceable as is an arbitration award;

(b) the expert enjoys no statutory immunity, although immunity may be conferred on him by the expert determination clause itself. Arbitrators, by contrast, enjoy a large measure of immunity under s 29 of the Arbitration Act 1996, unless their act or omission is shown to have been in bad faith;

(c) the expert determination clause must contain a minimum of information, the issues the expert must determine, how he is to be chosen and appointed and who is responsible for his fees. Arbitration, conversely, can be held to be binding simply by the parties stipulating that they wish their disputes to be resolved by arbitration. The statutory framework steps in to fill any omissions which parties have not considered.

### 1.7.4 Which form of dispute-resolution does adjudication most resemble?

Since adjudication produces an interim binding result, subject to review, it is to be distinguished markedly from mediation and conciliation. Adjudication is not arbitration and is not governed directly by the Arbitration Act 1996. However, the Housing Grants, Construction and Regeneration Act 1996 does introduce a framework illustrating how an adjudication should be conducted.

Adjudication clauses, in general, most closely resemble clauses for expert determination. However, a distinction must be made between adjudication clauses which are mandatory under the Housing Grants, Construction and Regeneration Act 1996, and those which have been voluntarily entered into, for example in international construction contracts.

In the latter case, relatively sophisticated parties consider and agree to a form of interim dispute-resolution. By contrast, adjudications under the 1996 Act may occur when neither party has considered adjudication at all or only in the most rudimentary fashion. In effect, a form of dispute-resolution is imposed, unlike any other 'alternative' form of dispute-resolution. In such cases, the Act and the detailed provisions provided in the scheme for construction contracts will apply.

### 1.7.5 Why does it matter which form of dispute-resolution adjudication most closely resembles?

In subsequent chapters, we will deal with the conduct of adjudications and enforcement of an adjudicator's decision. In discussing these aspects, we will draw on parallels both from arbitration and from the field of expert determination: the former because it is governed by a statutory framework and therefore has an Act of Parliament as its reference point (as do adjudications governed by the Housing Grants, Construction and Regeneration Act 1996) and the latter because adjudication clauses are generally expert determination clauses under another name, and the court pronouncements on the conduct of enforceability of expert's decisions may well provide some guidance on how adjudication awards will be enforced in the future.

# Chapter 2

## ADJUDICATION UNDER THE HOUSING GRANTS, CONSTRUCTION AND REGENERATION ACT 1996

### 2.1 THE RELEVANCE OF THE DATE OF THE CONSTRUCTION CONTRACT

Section 104(6) of the Housing Grants, Construction and Regeneration Act 1996 (the 1996 Act) states that it will apply to construction contracts which 'are entered into after the commencement of this part of the Act (1 May 1998)'. In the early stages, this may mean that, on a single project, some construction contracts will be subject to compulsory adjudication, while others will not. For example, an employer may engage a contractor before 1 May 1998. That contractor may subsequently enter into sub-contracts after that date. He may then be faced with an adjudication under a sub-contract, but have no similar statutory machinery in the main contract with his employer. If the main contractor wishes to avoid such a situation, he can either persuade his employer to include an adjudication in the main contract, or try to enter into the sub-contracts before 1 May 1998. He may, for example, deem that the sub-contracts were entered into by a certain date, which may be effective if it can be shown that there was indeed a contract at that date or, even if there is no formal contract, that the sub-contractor had commenced work. The date on the face of the relevant contract will be prima facie evidence of its actual date for these purposes. However, the courts will not countenance an attempt to backdate the contract long before any actual agreement between the main and sub-contractor in order to avoid application of Part II of the 1996 Act.

It often happens that construction contracts are not actually finalised and signed until some time after work has commenced, on occasions after work has been completed. In *Trollope & Colls Limited v Atomic Power Construction Limited*,[1] the defendants commenced work in June 1959 at the request of the plaintiffs and, on 11 April 1960, the form of general conditions of contract was agreed between the parties, the parties then being ad idem on the terms.

It was held that the parties had acted in negotiations on the understanding and in the anticipation that, if and whenever a contract was made, it would govern what was being done in the mean time.

It was stated that there was no principle of English law which provides that contract cannot have retrospective effect.

---

1    [1962] 3 All ER 1035.

If, therefore, work on a construction contract does commence before 1 May 1998, and the parties do have an intention that the written contract they eventually conclude is to govern what is done in the mean time, then the real start date of the contract will be before 1 May 1998 even though, in fact, the contract may be dated later.

## 2.2   DEFINITION OF CONSTRUCTION CONTRACT

Section 104(1) of the 1996 Act defines a construction contract as:

'... an agreement with a person for any of the following –

(a)   the carrying out of construction operations;
(b)   arranging for the carrying out of construction operations by others, whether under sub-contract to him or otherwise;
(c)   providing his own labour or the labour of others, for the carrying out of construction operations.'

By s 104(2), reference in Part II to a construction contract includes an agreement:

'(a)   to do architectural, design or surveying work, or
(b)   to provide advice on building, engineering, interior or exterior decoration or on the laying-out of landscape,'.

Section 105(1) of the 1996 Act goes on to define 'construction operations':

'... "construction operations" means, subject as follows, operations of any of the following descriptions –

(a)   construction, alteration, repair, maintenance, extension, demolition or dismantling of buildings, or structures forming, or to form, part of the land (whether permanent or not);
(b)   construction, alteration, repair, maintenance, extension, demolition or dismantling of any works forming, or to form, part of the land, including (without prejudice to the foregoing) walls, roadworks, power-lines, telecommunication apparatus, aircraft, runways, docks and harbours, railways, inland waterways, pipe-lines, reservoirs, water-mains, wells, sewers, industrial plant and installations for purposes of land drainage, coast protection or defence;
(c)   installation in any building or structure of fittings forming part of the land, including (without prejudice to the foregoing) systems of heating, lighting, air-conditioning, ventilation, power supply, drainage, sanitation, water supply or fire protection, or security or communication systems;
(d)   external or internal cleaning of buildings and structures, so far as carried out in the course of their construction, alteration, repair, extension or restoration;
(e)   operations which form an integral part of, or are preparatory to, or are for rendering complete, such operations as are previously described in this subsection, including site clearance, earth-moving, excavation, tunnelling and boring, laying of foundations, erection, maintenance or dismantling of scaffolding, site restoration, landscaping and the provision of roadways and other access works;
(f)   painting or decorating the internal or external surfaces of any building or structure.'

Many contracts provide for works, including both those listed above together with other services. Section 105(2)(d) goes on to make clear that where there is a contract for the manufacture, delivery and installation of:

'(i)   building or engineering components or equipment,
(ii)   materials, plant or machinery, or
(iii)  components for systems of heating, lighting, air-conditioning, ventilation, power supply, drainage, sanitation, water supply or fire protection, or for security or communications systems,'

these also fall within the definition of construction operations and are covered by the 1996 Act.

The definition of construction contracts is wide and all-embracing, and exclusions to it will be dealt with below. Two legalistic expressions are employed. First, s 105(1) relates to operations 'forming or to form, part of the land'. While it is clear that all types of works described are broadly 'construction works', this is included to emphasise that the definition relates to structures or buildings which are attached to the land and ownership in those buildings then passes to the owner of the land under English law. The Millennium Dome is not intended to be permanent, but does fall within the definition of construction operations. On the other hand, Portakabins are not usually structures which are intended to form part of the land. Section 29 of the Caravan Sites and Control of Development Act 1960 defines a caravan as 'any structure designed or adapted for human habitation which is capable of being moved from one place to another (whether under tow, or transported by a motor vehicle or trailer)'. It is arguable therefore that a contract solely for the supply and setting-up of Portakabins on a site will not be covered by the 1996 Act.

In *Potton Developments Ltd v Thompson and Another*,[1] the plaintiff manufactured pre-assembled bedrooms and en suite bathrooms, which were leased for seven years to an inn owner. The inn owner went into liquidation and the inn was sold. The subsequent purchasers (from the inn owner's mortgagees) argued that the units had become part of the land since they had been fixed to a prepared concrete slab, their roofs had been tiled together and the structures themselves had been tied to low retaining walls. Externally, they did appear to be permanent. Once a structure becomes part of the land, it becomes the property of the landowner whether or not he has in fact paid for it. The court held that the agreement showed that the installation was not intended to be permanent. When reviewing other cases, the judge made it clear that the paramount consideration was the purpose of the annexation, which in certain instances might be inferred from the way the structure was fixed or incorporated into the land. The greater the degree of annexation, the more difficult it will be for a supplier to argue that a structure has not become part of the land.

---

1    [1998] FLSCS 98.

## 2.3   CONSTRUCTION OPERATIONS

The 1996 Act applies to all construction operations undertaken in England, Wales or Scotland.[1] Construction operations are widely defined to include professional design work by engineers or architects. For example, a London-based interior designer working for a British-based client on the refurbishment of a hotel in Spain would not be able to invoke the 1996 Act and seek adjudication of a dispute since the operation is in Spain and not in the UK. This is the case even if the contract provided that the laws of England should apply to the project (see s 104(7)).

In many contracts the parties choose the law which is to apply and, accordingly, the contract will be interpreted in accordance with that law. In the majority of construction contracts the applicable law is that of the country in which the project is to be undertaken, since generally the client is from that country. This, however, is not always the case. Contracts for the construction of consular or diplomatic buildings are usually not subject to the local law.

However, even if the law chosen to govern the contract is not the law of the country where the project is undertaken, the laws of that country will apply to such issues as planning, building regulations and health and safety. The 1996 Act seems to fall into the same category, which means that adjudication could be available to a designer, architect or engineer who, for example, is based outside Great Britain, but whose work is in relation to a construction project located within Great Britain. Although it is likely that the applicable law of the contract in such a case would be English or Scottish law, it is possible that another law may be chosen or implied.[2] Even so, it appears that the designer, architect or engineer could avail himself of the 1996 Act and seek an adjudication in the event of a dispute.

Geographically, construction operations in England, Wales and Scotland are covered by the 1996 Act, but not the Channel Islands or the Isle of Man. The 1996 Act does not extend to the territorial waters of Scotland, England, Wales and Northern Ireland and, as such, offshore construction operations are not covered. These are most likely to be oil and gas extraction operations which are, in any event, excluded under the provisions of s 105(2) (see **2.4.4** below).

---

1    A separate but similar scheme applies in Scotland.

2    Where the parties to a contract have not expressly chosen the applicable law, and the contract is between parties situated within the European Union, the provisions of the EEC Convention on the Law Applicable to Contractual Obligations will apply. The Convention applies a test of the 'characteristic performance of the contract'. In a contract for design services, the characteristic performance is where the actual design work is undertaken, which may mean an applicable law which is not the law of the country in which the project is located.

## 2.4   CONSTRUCTION CONTRACTS NOT COVERED BY THE 1996 ACT

### 2.4.1   Contracts for residential occupiers

Section 106 of the 1996 Act states that the Act does not apply to a construction contract which relates principally to operations on a dwelling which a residential occupier occupies or intends to occupy as his residence. The section goes onto state that 'dwelling' means a house or a flat, but not a building of which a flat forms part. The 1996 Act makes the distinction between horizontally divided flats forming self-contained premises and vertically separated premises such as houses in a terrace.

The 1996 Act does not apply to the owner of a house or flat who engages a contractor to undertake repair, renovation or alteration, nor to a contract for the construction of a house which will then be occupied by the employer. The significant aspect of this exception is the *occupation*, or the *intention to occupy* by the employer. As such, the 1996 Act will apply where renovation or repair is carried out on a house which the owner does not occupy or intend to occupy.

In many cases, occupation will be clear, for example when the occupier is actually living in the dwelling while works are being undertaken, or moves out for a short period to enable renovation works to be undertaken. However, if the building has never been occupied by one of the parties, or is being newly built, determining an intention to occupy may be more difficult. The nature of the contract may make it clear that the particular wishes of the party relating, for example, to finishes and internal fit-outs may indicate conclusively that this is a dwelling he intends to occupy. Less clear are those circumstances where the intention to occupy is uncertain or changes during the course of the construction contract.

In *Cunliffe v Goodman*,[1] the tenant wanted to avoid paying for his failure properly to repair the building during the currency of his lease on the ground that the landlord had the intention of pulling down the building. The court ruled that the tenant had to show that the landlord had a definitive intention, or had arrived at a decision to demolish. Since a decision to demolish was dependent on the terms of the planning permission imposed by the local authority, which were not yet known, it was held that there was no definitive intention.

Applying these principals, a party to a construction contract who can show an intention to occupy (or reoccupy) at the time the contract was entered into, can exclude the application of the 1996 Act.

### 2.4.2   Intention to occupy

If a dispute occurs over whether one party to the construction contract intends to occupy or reoccupy the property, can the adjudicator rule upon this issue?

---

1    [1950] 1 All ER 720.

Section 108 of the 1996 Act provides that a party to a construction contract has the right to refer a dispute or difference to adjudication. A contract for the renewal or construction of a dwelling falls within the definition of a construction contract, and is excluded only by virtue of s 106. If there is a dispute over whether or not the exclusion applies, this, it is submitted, is itself a difference or dispute under a construction contract. It may be argued that this is instead an issue of jurisdiction. Does the adjudicator have the capacity to decide such an issue? Section 30 of the Arbitration Act 1996 permits an arbitrator (among other things) specifically to rule on whether or not there is a valid arbitration agreement. Thus, s 30 embodies a well-established and internationally recognised doctrine that an arbitral tribunal is able to rule upon its own competence.

In Chapter 1, we discussed the nature of adjudication, and whether it more closely resembles arbitration, expert determination, or, being a creature of statute, whether it is an entirely new means of dispute-resolution. In practice, this issue will arise where the construction contract makes no provision for adjudication and, as such, the Scheme for Construction Contracts (the Scheme), a statutory code made under the 1996 Act, will apply.[1] The Scheme does not specifically confer upon the nominated adjudicator the power to rule upon his own competence. Paragraph 13, however, gives the adjudicator wide scope to 'take the initiative in ascertaining the facts and the law necessary to determine the dispute'. Arguably, the adjudicator can use this power to ascertain whether or not the construction contract is excluded from the provisions of the 1996 Act.

### 2.4.3 Contracts of employment

#### *Contracts for services or contracts of service?*

Section 104(4) of the Housing Grants, Construction and Regeneration Act 1996 states that construction contracts do not include contracts of employment as defined by the Employment Rights Act 1996. The Employment Rights Act 1996 defines contracts of employment as contracts for service or apprenticeship whether oral or in writing. In employment law, an important distinction is made between contracts of service, where the party peforming the service does so under the direction of the party paying for it, and contracts for services, where, although one party performs services for another for payment, the relationship is not one of employer/employee. The Employment Rights Act 1996 does not apply to contracts of service and any disputes must be dealt with either under the machinery provided for in the employment contract itself or, ultimately, by the industrial tribunal or the courts. Whether there is a contract of service or a contract for services is a question of fact. Over the years the courts have used a number of criteria with varying degrees of emphasis, for example the control test, the economic reality test and the organisation test. A simple test suggested by the Employment Appeals Tribunal in 1981 was to ask 'are you your own boss?' If so, a contract for services exists. In the contract of the construction industry, this is an

---

1    Scheme for Construction Contracts (England and Wales) Regulations 1998, SI 1998/649.

especially pertinent issue. If a designer is engaged for a weekly fee to work in the design office of a contractor, is he an independent sub-contractor or an employee? In the former case, the 1996 Act will apply, in the latter case, it will not.

In *Express & Echo Publications Limited v Tanton*,[1] the Court of Appeal ruled that it was necessary for a contract of employment to contain an obligation on the part of the employee to provide services personally. A contract which allows services to be carried out by a person other than the contractor is a contract for services and not a contract of service. Mr Tanton had been an employee of the company, but was made redundant and subsequently taken on as a driver under an 'agreement for service' which provided that, in the event that he was unable or unwilling to perform the services personally, he should arrange at his own expense entirely for another suitable person to perform the services. The law now recognises unambiguously that a contract of employment involves mutual trust and confidence: *Malik v Bank of Credit and Commerce International SA*.[2] The parties intended that Mr Tanton should be a self-employed contractor and the absence of holiday and sickness pay which a tribunal chairman had found to be pointers to a contract of service, was in no way inconsistent with a contract for services.

## 2.4.4   Operations excluded by the 1996 Act

Pursuant to s 105(2), the following are not construction operations within the meaning of the 1996 Act and are not, therefore, required to remit disputes to adjudication:

'(a)   drilling for, or extraction of, oil or natural gas;

(b)   extraction (whether by underground or surface working) of minerals; tunnelling or boring, or construction of underground works for this purpose;

(c)   assembly, installation or demolition of plant or machinery, or erection or demolition of steelwork for the purpose of supporting or providing access to plant or machinery, on a site where the primary activity is –

(i)   nuclear processing, power generation, or water or effluent treatment, or

(ii)   the production, transmission, processing or bulk storage (other than warehousing) of chemicals, pharmaceuticals, oil, gas, steel or food and drink;

(d)   manufacture or delivery to site of –

(i)   building or engineering components or equipment,

(ii)   materials, plant or machinery, or

(iii)   components for systems of heating, lighting, air-conditioning, ventilation, power supply, drainage, sanitation, water supply or fire protection, or for security or communications systems;

except under a contract which also provides for their installation;

(e)   the making, installation and repair of artistic works, being sculptures, murals and other works which are wholly artistic in nature.'

---

1     (1999) *The Times*, 7 April.
2     [1997] ICR 606.

It is important to note that extraction is excluded from the 1996 Act, but tunnelling, boring or other underground works which are not for the purpose of extraction are not excluded.

Under s 105(2)(c), the nuclear processing power generation, water effluent treatment or the processing of chemical pharmaceuticals, oil, gas, steel, food or drink must be the primary activity. If these activities merely form part of other activities which are not excluded, the 1996 Act will apply. Warehousing is an exception, so that the construction of a warehouse for the bulk storage of any of the above-mentioned would be subject to the 1996 Act.

Although a contract for the manufacture or delivery to a construction site of certain materials is not subject to the 1996 Act, it will become subject if the contract includes installation of those components.

Section 105(3) provides that the Secretary of State can order, amend or appeal operations which are defined as construction operations, and those which are not. Section 106(1)(b) (which excludes residential occupiers) states that adjudication and payment provisions do not apply 'to any other description of construction contract excluded from the operation of this Part [of the Act] by Order of the Secretary of State'. On 6 March 1998, the first Order was issued, and is reproduced in full in Appendix 1.[1] It excludes from the 1996 Act agreements under statute, contracts entered into under the private finance initiative, finance agreements and development agreements. These are set out in detail at **2.4.5–2.4.8** inclusive.

## 2.4.5    Agreements under statute

The following agreements are expressly not construction contracts:

(a)  agreements under s 38 (adoption of highways) and s 278 (agreements to execute works) of the Highways Act 1980;
(b)  agreements under ss 106, 106A or 299A of the Town and Country Planning Act 1990;
(c)  agreements to adopt a sewer, drain or sewage disposal works under s 104 of the Water Industries Act 1991;
(d)  an externally financed development agreement within the meaning of s 1 of the National Health Service (Private Finance) Act 1997.

## 2.4.6    Private finance initiative

Construction contracts entered into under the private finance initiative (PFI) are excluded if certain conditions are fulfilled, as follows:

(a)  the contract must contain a statement that it is entered into under the PFI or, as the case may be, under a project applying similar principles;
(b)  the consideration (usually the payment of money) under the PFI is to be determined, at least in part, by:

---

1    Construction Contracts (England and Wales) Exclusion Order 1998, SI 1998/648.

(i)      the standards obtained in the performance of a service, the provision of which is the principal purpose, or one of the principal purposes, for which the building or structure is constructed,

(ii)      the extent, rate or intensity of use of all or any part of the building or structure in question, or

(iii)      the right to operate any facility in connection with the building or structure in question;

(c)     one of the parties to the contract is a minister of the Crown, a government department or other bodies whose accounts are examined, certified or audited by the Comptroller and Auditor General, or auditors appointed by the Audit Commission, nationalised industries and other public authorities and the governing bodies and trustees of voluntary schools, or companies or bodies owned by any of the above.

Article 4(2)(c) of the Exclusion Order lists the types of contract under statute is reasonably clear, and agreements will be with highway authorities, planning authorities, water authorities and NHS trusts. The exclusion will apply only to the party contracting directly with those bodies, and not to subsidiary agreements with architects, engineers, surveyors, contractors or sub-contractors.

PFI exclusions will apply if the amount of payment is dependent upon a variable factor, as described above. For example, a PFI construction contract for the erection of a bridge which is to be paid for from either the right to collect tolls from the public or shadow tolls to be paid by the highway authority depending upon the number of users would be excluded. However, a PFI construction contract to build an office block which is to be occupied for the whole term of the agreement by a government department which pays a certain sum per month or per year, would not contain one of the variable factors and, as such, would not be excluded.

Only the party contracting with one of the above bodies can exclude the 1996 Act from the construction contract. Engineers, architects, surveyors and contractors who are not direct parties to the PFI consortium (not merely shareholders in a company formed for that purpose) cannot exclude the 1996 Act from their respective agreements. Such persons will instead be able to insist on adjudications, as well as the inclusion of the payment provisions, which are dealt with in Chapter 5.

## 2.4.7   Finance agreements

Financial agreements are defined in art 5(2) of the Exclusion Order as contracts for the following:

'(a)    any contract of insurance;

(b)    any contract under which the principal obligations include the formation or dissolution of a company, unincorporated association or partnership;

(c)    any contract under which the principal obligations include the creation or transfer of securities or any right or interest in securities;

(d)    any contract under which the principal obligations include the lending of money;

(e)   any contract under which the principal obligations include an undertaking by a person to be responsible as surety for the debt or default of another person, including a fidelity bond, advance payment bond, retention bond or performance bond.'

The Order aims to exclude from the 1996 Act all bonds and guarantees from its provisions, including those where the guarantor[1] has the right to shoulder the obligation of the principal[2] to complete the works. This is not to say, however, that the parties cannot agree to adjudication under a guarantee. The ICE form of default bond provides that if a call on the bond is challenged, the dispute may be referred to an adjudicator appointed under the construction contract.

## 2.4.8   Collateral warranties

The 1998 Exclusion Order does not directly include collateral warranties, under which the party who is to perform the service, or undertake the contract works, agrees to have contractual responsibility to parties other than those with whom the party has originally contracted to execute the works. Under collateral warranties produced by the British Property Federation (BPF), which are approved by the Association of Consulting Engineers (ACE), the Royal Institution of Chartered Surveyors (RICS) and the Royal Institute of British Architects (RIBA), the engineer, architect, surveyor or contractor agrees to enter into a contract with the future purchaser and/or tenants of a building. When that new contractual link is formed by virtue of the collateral warranty, will 'construction operations' be undertaken? Arguably, this is not the intention since the collateral warranty is likely to be called upon only after construction work has finished. The 1996 Act states, however, that adjudication can be commenced at any time.[3] Is the beneficiary of the collateral warranty a party to a construction contract,[4] in other words are they in contract with somebody who is carrying out construction operations. However, where a similar form of bond is entered into with parties who finance the project (CoWa/F),[5] the position may be clearer. A finance company reserves a right to enter into a direct contract of employment with the consultant if the latter gives notice that it is about to terminate its agreement, or the former gives notice that it has terminated its finance agreement with the employer (but nevertheless wishes to employ the consultant to complete the project). Once either of these events occurs, the finance company steps into the shoes of the former employer and will, in effect, be entering into a construction contract, ie it will be engaged in construction operations as defined by the 1996 Act, and the 1996 Act will apply. Similar provisions exist in the collateral warranty

---

1   The guarantor is often a bank or insurance company from whom a guarantee or bond is procured by the principal.
2   This is usually a contractor, but could, in certain circumstances, be an employer.
3   The 1996 Act, s 108(1)–(2)(a); see Appendix 1.
4   The 1996 Act, s 104; see Appendix 1.
5   Collateral warranty for use where a warranty is to be given to a company providing finance for a proposed development.

(MCWa/F)[1] which is provided by a main contractor to a company providing finance.

## 2.4.9 Rights of third parties

The Contract (Rights of Third Parties) Act 1999 (the 1999 Act) is estimated to be in force some time early in the year 2000, six months after its enactment. It will apply to all contracts entered into after that date. The object of the Act is to reform the rule of privity of contract under which a person can only enforce a contract if he is a party to it. The rule is, of course, the principal reason for the existence of collateral warranties. The 1999 Act provides for third parties to be granted rights to enforce terms of the contract, either where this is expressly provided for in the contract or where the contract 'purports' to confer a benefit on that third party. The third party must be identified in the contract either by class or by name. There are a number of contracts which are excluded from the provisions of the 1999 Act, but construction contracts, as defined by the 1996 Act, are not excluded. The issue therefore arises, if a third party obtains the benefit of the terms of the construction contract does this include the right to refer to adjudication any disputes which may arise? Paradoxically, this issue has already arisen in relation to arbitration clauses in contracts. Should third parties who acquire benefits under the 1996 Act be able to benefit from such arbitration clauses, but at the same time not be bound to arbitrate in the event of dispute, on the theory that the 1996 Act is there to confer benefits not burdens? The Law Commission, in its report in 1996, concluded that arbitration clauses should be excluded from the scope of the 1999 Act. This exclusion was not, however, included in the Bill presented to Parliament.

The same consideration will apply to those who acquire benefits of terms of a construction contract. Will they be entitled to refer any dispute that they have to adjudication? The 1999 Act specifically states in s 1(5) that:

> 'For the purpose of exercising his right to enforce a term of the contract, there shall be available to the third party any remedy that would have been available to him in an action for breach of contract if he had been a party to the contract . . .'

As with collateral warranties, we suggest that the statutory right to adjudicate, for instance, when the right is not an express term of the contract, will only arguably apply if construction operations are on-going. However, if the right to adjudicate is expressed and is not limited to, say, the two contracting parties, then the third party could benefit from such a clause.

Unlike the 1996 Act, those drafting constructing contracts can exclude the rights of third parties, or limit the terms of the contract which should benefit third parties. For example, they could exclude the right of any third party to benefit from an arbitration clause. Can the right to adjudicate be excluded from the rights that benefit the third party if it is envisaged that the third party should not benefit from the contract once 'construction operations' have been concluded? If,

---

1    Collateral warranty for use where a warranty is to be given to a company providing finance (Funder) for the proposed building works by a main contractor.

however, there is a possibility of construction operations continuing whilst the third party is to benefit from the terms of the contract, then the right to adjudicate is conferred by statute and it does not appear possible to exclude the right of that third party to adjudicate.

The premise that an adjudication clause is mandatory only for construction contracts where construction operations are actually being undertaken (rather than being completed some time previously) is based on a purposive interpretation of the legislation. A literal interpretation might well suggest that the right to adjudication persists long after the works are completed and could be exercised by a third party who was never party to those construction operations.

### 2.4.10 Development agreements

Development agreements are excluded from the provisions of the 1996 Act if they come within the following definition: the contract must include provision for the grant or disposal of a relevant interest in land upon which the principal construction operations to which the contract relates are to take place. This can include a freehold, or a leasehold for a period which is to expire no later than 12 months after the completion of the construction operations.

### 2.4.11 Assignments and novations

Most standard form building contracts and consultancy appointments permit the employer to assign the benefit of the contract. Such assignment usually requires the consent of the contractor/consultant, which consent cannot be unreasonably withheld. If the contract is a construction contract as defined by the 1996 Act and entered into after 1 May 1998, the 1996 Act will continue to apply to the new party or assignee. If, however, the original contract was entered into before 1 May 1998, a mere assignment will not give rise to the application of the 1996 Act since the same contract continues in being. As with all assignments,[1] the employer can assign the benefit of the contract, but he cannot escape the burden. In the unlikely event that an adjudicator's monetary decision is not met by the new employer, application could be made to the old employer for its payment. Such recourse may be of use to the payee in the event of the new employer's insolvency. However, the same defences to payment available to the new employer would also be available to the old employer.

The terms of an assignment must be examined. If assignment in fact amounts to a novation, the former employer has no further obligations. In such circumstances, it is as if there has been a complete substitution of the new employer for the old, and a new contract is consequently formed. Therefore, if the original contract was entered into before 1 May 1998, but the novation occurred after that date, the new contract may be subject to the 1996 Act.

---

1  Excepting the assignment of certain leases.

## 2.5   CONTRACTS MUST BE IN WRITING

Section 107 of the 1996 Act makes it clear that it is applicable only to contracts in writing. The definition is wide and includes contracts merely 'evidenced in writing' or recorded by 'any means to include an exchange of written submissions in adjudication proceedings where the existence of a contract is not denied'.

In the rare cases where a construction contract is not in writing nor evidenced or recorded, a party threatened with adjudication has limited options if he wishes to avoid adjudication and, consequently, enforcement of the payment provisions. By virtue of s 107(5) it is not open to him to make a submission in writing to the adjudicator to the effect that adjudication does not apply since this is an oral contract. The mere fact of making the submission converts what was an oral contract into a written contract. This also precludes a written submission to the arbitrator that he does not have jurisdiction to hear the dispute. Generally, such a submission can be framed in a way which does not admit the jurisdiction of the arbitrator, even though it is being made to the arbitrator.

Therefore, the party must either make oral submissions to the adjudicator, or refuse to honour the adjudicator's decision, an option which is dealt with in more detail in Chapter 5.

## 2.6   DISPUTES REFERABLE TO ADJUDICATION

### 2.6.1   Periods within which adjudication may be used

Section 108(1) of the 1996 Act gives the parties to a construction contract the right to refer a dispute or difference under the contract to adjudication. No limit is placed on the time period within which the dispute or difference must be referred, nor on the type of dispute.

It is theoretically possible for a disupte to be referred to adjudication soon after the construction contract has been entered into or, conversely, long after the works have been completed unless one accepts the premise, explored at **2.4.10** that adjudication is available only during the currency of 'construction operations'. Adjudication (both domestic and international) has been seen as a means of quickly resolving disputes as they arise only during the course of the contract works. However, no such limitation appears in the 1996 Act.

Interestingly, the Scheme for Construction Contracts contains a qualification on the type of disputes upon which the adjudicator can decide. Under art 20(a) the adjudicator may

> 'open up, revise and review any decision taken or any certificate given by any person referred to in the contract *unless* the contract states that the decision or certificate is final and conclusive, ...' (emphasis added).

Some commentators have suggested that this will encourage drafters of construction contracts to word them in such a way that most, if not all, of the decisions of the certifier under the contract are made 'final'. The Scheme was introduced by way of the Scheme for Construction Contracts (England and Wales) Regulations, SI 1998/649. The limitation in the Scheme appears to be contrary to at least the letter of the 1996 Act, and whether anyone or any body acting on behalf of contractors or sub-contractors would be prepared to launch a challenge to the presumption of regularity of this limitation must be a moot point. In order to succeed, it would be necessary to show special circumstances for the limitation imposed by the statutory instrument to be questioned.

Since any decision of the adjudicator is subject to review (unless the parties to the contract choose to make it binding), whether the parties consider it worthwhile to refer disputes to adjudication after the works are completed will depend on the circumstances. A party may consider it an advantage that an adjudicator must make a decision within the relatively short period of time prescribed by the 1996 Act, rather than referring the dispute to the courts of arbitration, where a decision is likely to be rendered only months or, indeed, years later.

This is likely to be true where there are sums of money due at the end of the works. Whether it is advantageous to launch a complicated claim in adjudication alleging negligence and consequential damages after the works are complete is quite different, precisely because the short time period does not allow sufficient time to examine such issues.

## 2.6.2 Disputes and cross-claims

If a party to a construction contract has a dispute then it can be referred to adjudication, but when is a dispute or difference constituted? If one party is making a claim, does that claim have to be fully constituted before a dispute can arise? It is submitted that it does not. If there is a clear difference of opinion then it does not matter that the final consequences of that difference have yet to be formulated. It may even be the case that the dispute arises before the claimant has a fully constituted cause of action. Suppose, for example, that a contractor has submitted his application for payment which has prompted notices from the employer indicating set-off or abatement. Whether or not the notices served by the employer comply with the payment provisions (examined in Chapter 5), it is open to the claimant to refer the dispute to an adjudicator before the final date for payment. In *Remac Construction Company Limited v JE Lesser (Properties) Limited*,[1] Forbes J ruled that whilst a condition precedent to an action in the courts may not have arisen, such a condition precedent did not apply to an arbitration.

Once a notice of adjudication has been served and the matter referred to the adjudicator, can the respondent raise cross-claims and should these be considered by the adjudicator?

Any cross-claims, if they are to be considered at all, must arise under the construction contract, otherwise they are outside the jurisdiction of the adjudicator. A dispute on a different contract between the parties could not be

---

1     [1975] 2 Lloyd's Rep 430.

considered by the adjudicator (although a court may suspend enforcement of an adjudicator's award pending determination of this other dispute).

In the event that the cross-claims be expressed as a defence, for example, where the sums claimed are not due because works have not been executed properly, then it should be allowed. The real issue is when a dispute arises which is then referred to a nominated adjudicator and only then does the respondent raise a cross-claim which was not identified in the original dispute.

It is submitted that in those circumstances the adjudicator should not entertain the cross-claim, unless of course the referring party agrees. Mustill and Boyd[1] clearly take the view that an arbitrator in those circumstances should not entertain the cross-claim.

The TeCSA Rules of Adjudication, rule 11(ii), do give the adjudicator power to consider 'any further matters which the Adjudicator determines must be included in order that the adjudication may be effective and/or meaningful'. The CEDR rules state that the adjudicator shall decide the matters referred to him.

This could be construed as meaning the matters raised in the referring parties notice of referral. By contrast, the ICE and CIC rules state that the matters set out in the notice of adjudication are to be determined by the adjudicator, together with other matters agreed between the parties. The Scheme for Construction Contracts (England and Wales) Regulations 1998 speak simply of the adjudicator deciding 'the matters in dispute'. He may take into account any other matters which the parties to the dispute agree should be within the scope of the adjudication or which are matters under the contract which he considers are necessarily connected with the dispute. In order to ascertain what is in dispute, some adjudicators call for the correspondence that has passed between the parties. If the respondent is raising an issue which does not feature in the correspondence, then the adjudicator may well consider that he will not deal with it.

Despite the apparent latitude given in the TeCSA rules, we submit that an adjudicator should be slow to allow a cross-claim which is not part of the original dispute. To do so may impede the progress of the current adjudication. In any event, the respondent can always launch his own adjudication. Given an adjudication's short duration, this is not the burden it would be in, say, an arbitration.

## 2.6.3 Parallel proceedings

In certain circumstances where a dispute has been referred to arbitration, or court proceedings have been issued, the other party may decide, again for tactical reasons, to seek an adjudicator's decision on the dispute. An analogous situation is where one party seeks to litigate the dispute while the other party wants to have the matter dealt with by arbitration under an arbitration clause in the contract. Since the coming into force of s 9 of the Arbitration Act 1996 the courts have no

---

1    Mustill and Boyd *Commercial Arbitration* 2nd edn (Butterworths, 1989) p 131.

option in these circumstances but to stay the legal proceedings and allow the arbitration to proceed. However, adjudication is intended only to provide an interim decision, which is then reviewable (if the parties agree) either by the courts or by an arbitrator. In practice, this apparent ability to have parallel sets of proceedings will not last for much longer than the 35 days from initiation to decision.

### 2.6.4 Time-limit for decision

An adjudication must be concluded within 35 days of the initiation of the process (unless the parties agree to extend the time). A period of just over one month, in terms of litigation or indeed the majority of arbitrations, is a relatively short period. Nevertheless, if a decision is rendered, it is binding and enforceable.

### 2.6.5 Dispute review boards

The adjudication provisions in the JCT Domestic and Nominated Sub-Contract Forms were limited to challenging the main contractor's set-off, ie they were confined to disputes over payments of money. The adjudication provisions in the New Engineering Contract (NEC) (now the New Engineering and Construction Contract) encompassed 'any dispute arising under or in connection with this contract'. Contracts which include a provision referring any disputes to dispute review boards (DRBs) do not limit the powers of those boards purely to questions of payment or non-payment of money due. The continuing involvement of DRBs during the course of the project makes them well-suited to resolving technical disputes as and when they arise.

## 2.7 CRITICISMS OF ADJUDICATION

Concern has been expressed by some commentators over mandatory adjudication in all construction contracts, and this concern has focused on a number of issues.

The definition of a construction contract includes professional appointments who have not previously had, nor presumably seen the need, for adjudication as a form of dispute-resolution.

The scope of adjudication means that any dispute can be referred to an adjudicator. The contractor can therefore challenge a decision of the supervising officer on a technical issue and attain a decision from an adjudicator within 35 days. The adjudicator's decision may be entirely contrary to the professional opinion of the supervising officer, who may consider that to abide by it will impugn the design or structure of the building or project. If the designer advises his client to comply with the adjudicator's decision (against his better judgment), and the building develops faults subsequently as a result, he cannot argue in his defence that he advised on the basis of the adjudicator's decision, since the adjudicator's liability to the parties is limited under the 1996 Act to acts or omissions in bad faith, and the employer is still likely to pursue the consultant.

Since the period of time in which the adjudicator must come to a decision is relatively short, complicated disputes referred to adjudication may not receive the detailed examination they merit. Although the adjudicator's decision can be reviewed, this will lead to injustice until a final ruling by a judge or arbitrator can be made. This criticism is particularly pertinent where the decision of the adjudicator is, in effect, final. Where, for example, a contractor challenges an engineer's direction that the foundations of a building should be re-laid, and the adjudicator's decision supports the view of the contractor, it will be too late three to four years subsequently to have the decision reviewed and possibly reversed by a court or technically qualified arbitrator since the building will be completed and the foundations inaccessible.

Whether injustice results will depend largely on the importance which adjudicators, and the courts and arbitrators that are called upon to enforce his decision, apply to s 108(3) of the 1996 Act, which states:

> 'The contract shall provide that the decision of the adjudicator is binding until the dispute is finally determined by legal proceedings, by arbitration (if the contract provides for arbitration or the parties otherwise agree to agree to arbitration) or by agreement. The parties may agree to accept the decision of the adjudicator as finally determining the dispute.'

It is clear that the decision of the adjudicator is an *interim* decision, unless and until the parties agree to accept it as final. It is suggested that an arbitrator or court called upon to enforce an adjudicator's decision should be wary of such a decision which, although on the face of it is an interim decision, in reality decides matters finally. If, for example, an adjudicator's decision requires a contractor to make a payment to a sub-contractor who is on the point of going into liquidation, in practice the decision of the adjudicator is final since any review has been precluded by the sub-contractor's insolvency.

## 2.7.1 Stakeholders

The JCT Domestic and Nominated Sub-Contract Forms provided that an adjudicator could direct that a sum in dispute be paid to a stakeholder. This device was used particularly where there was doubt over whether the recipient of the payment would be able to repay the sum in question if the adjudicator's decision was revised subsequently. No such provision appears either in the 1996 Act or the statutory Scheme for Construction Contracts, nor, indeed, in any other schemes that we examine in Chapter 3. Some commentators have suggested that an adjudicator who orders payment to a stakeholder is avoiding the issue and is not, in effect, rendering a decision since the impoverished payee's immediate benefit is minimal. It is submitted that a decision that a sum be paid to a stakeholder should be made only on the clearest of grounds, with consideration being given to directing that only part of the money should go to the stakeholder, with the remainder to the payee.

## 2.7.2   Suspension

The Standing Commitee for Structural Safety (SCOSS) has expressed concerns[1] that a decision concerning safety may be given by an adjudicator unqualified to give such a decision, thus compromising the safety of the project. They are also concerned about the right to suspend work[2] if sums due under the construction contract are not paid. They consider that such a suspension could introduce risks to structural safety, for example if a tunnelling contractor were to suddenly stop a drive into soft ground.

## 2.8   CRITICISMS ANSWERED

Concerns over adjudication are real, but they can be overstated. First, they do not take full account of the work to date of DRBs, and their power to deal with a wide range of disputes. Experience seems to suggest that adjudicators' decisions are largely respected. However, appointees to DRBs have the opportunity to become well acquainted with the contract before a dispute arises, and, as such, are not as hindered by time-limits when deciding issues.

The fact that the appointment of construction consultants is now subject to statutory adjudication is a radical change, but can be seen as recognition of modern day realities. The principle of an architect or engineer administering the contract in an impartial manner is eroding. In addition, many design professionals are today not employed by the owner of the building or scheme but by design and build contractors. In this position, they can be as vulnerable as sub-contractors to disputes over money. An employer can invariably raise sufficient allegations of deficient design and/or delay to defeat any prospect of summary judgment on a claim for outstanding fees.

As far as challenges to the decisions of a supervising officer are concerned, an adjudicator who comes to a decision contrary to the professional opinion of the supervising officer presents a choice: either the supervising officer accepts the adjudicator's decision, or he maintains his position. For example, an architect condemns a wall because the cavity has been filled with mortar droppings. The contractor concedes that there are droppings but contends that the problem is not as serious as the architect believes and can be rectified without demolition. The architect insists on demolition, and the contractor refers the matter to an adjudicator. If the adjudicator rules in favour of the contractor, what stance should the architect adopt? If the architect remains convinced of the correctness of his original decision, he should issue a variation to the contract requiring the demolition of the wall. It follows that the contractor will be paid for this demolition and, as such, should be satisfied. The issue will then be re-examined in an arbitration or by the courts. The example we have given involves the danger of impairing thermal insulation and possibly allowing damp penetration; it is not a

---

1    The SCOSS 12th Report published by the Institution of Structural Engineers.
2    Section 112(1) of the 1996 Act; see also Appendix 1.

safety issue. The same principle, however, should hold good when safety issues are involved. It would be an unwise adjudicator who gave an instruction that a particular thing should be done on site. If called upon to do so, he will give a decision as to whether particular work conforms to the requirement of the contract; in doing so, he will no doubt be slow to supplant the opinion of the consultant who has presumably carefully considered the issue before making the initial decision. If, then, the consulting engineer, or whoever has a responsibility for safety, truly considers that what the adjudicator has decided is not safe, he should then issue an instruction for a contractor to be paid to do what he directs.

Effectively, the intervention of the adjudicator reverses the traditional position. Previously, the rights of a contractor to refer a decision of the supervising officer to arbitration before practical completion were limited. An aggrieved contractor, certainly under the JCT Standard Form of Contract, could pursue his remedy only after practical completion. Now the onus is upon an employer who disagrees with the adjudicator's decision to pursue a review of the adjudicator's decision through either arbitration or the courts. If the above example of the wall is taken, the contractor would previously have had to bear the cost of demolishing the wall until the final decision of an arbitrator. Henceforth, if the adjudicator's decision is favourable to the contractor, the employer will have to bear the cost of the demolition until the arbitration. Suspending work on a contract is not a new concept. Most contractors do it as a matter of course each evening, at weekends and for the two weeks at Christmas. The contractor knows he must make the site safe before departing. Before exercising this right under the 1996 Act, the contractor has, of course, to give seven days' notice to his employer. The contractor, or indeed the consultant who has not been paid, has the right to suspend his obligations *to the party by whom payment should have been made* but this does not absolve the contractor from his duty of safety to the world at large.[1]

Concerns of 'ambush', for example where the claimant has unlimited time to prepare a complicated case, which he then springs on an unsuspecting defendant who has a maximum of only 28 days before the adjudicator reaches a decision, can be overstated. First, a dispute of this complexity will probably have been canvassed between the parties beforehand, particularly if it arises during the course of the contract. Complex disputes that are ultimately litigated or arbitrated upon involve events which occurred many months, if not years before, since when the contract has progressed and other factors have come into play. Secondly, such a scenario makes it very unlikely that an adjudicator can act 'impartially' as he is required to do by s 108(2)(e) of the 1996 Act. If the claimant presents a detailed claim and then refuses to agree to an extension of time, this has the effect of denying the respondent the opportunity properly to reply, and hence the ability of the adjudicator to come to an impartial decision is hampered.

Few commentators doubt that an expert called upon to decide a dispute must act fairly. Whether this goes further and imposes upon the adjudicator a duty to act in

---

1    Article by Roger Sainsbury entitled 'Safety and the Construction Act' in *New Civil Engineer*, dated 21 May 1998.

accordance with the rules of natural justice is another matter entirely, which is dealt with in more detail in Chapter 4. However, an adjudicator faced with a detailed claim, where there is no realistic prospect of the respondent having the opportunity to reply, is clearly being asked to act unfairly. If the claimant is warned by the adjudicator that more time is required, and fails to accede to this request, the adjudicator can reject the claim on the basis that in the circumstances he is unable to discharge his duty to act impartially. If he chooses to proceed to a positive decision, based effectively only on the evidence of the claimant, his decision runs the real risk of not being enforceable, which will be addressed in more detail in Chapters 4 and 5. This applies particularly where the contract has been completed, since the right to suspend work on the contract where payment is not made pursuant to an adjudicator's decision is no longer an effective remedy.

# Chapter 3

## THE RULES OF ADJUDICATION EXAMINED

### 3.1 INTRODUCTION

In order to comply with s 108[1] of the Housing Grants, Construction and Regeneration Act 1996 (the 1996 Act), a construction contract must provide that the adjudication procedure conforms with the criteria set out in that section. If the contract does not comply, or does not make reference to a set of rules which comply, the statutory Scheme for Construction Contracts (the Scheme) made under the 1996 Act[2] will be applied. The omission of only one of the criteria is sufficient for the Scheme to apply. The criteria consist of eight requirements as follows.

#### 3.1.1 Notice of intention to refer a dispute – s 108(2)(a)

A party has a right to give notice at any time of his intention to refer a dispute or difference arising under the contract to adjudication. Whether this means that a contract needs to spell out that an adjudication can be commenced 'at any time' or whether it is sufficient not to fetter this right is debatable. However, for the avoidance of doubt, the contract drafter should include a positive statement to this effect.

#### 3.1.2 The timetable for appointment – s 108(2)(b)

The adjudication procedure must provide a timetable for securing the appointment of the adjudicator, and referral to him of the dispute within seven days of such appointment. An adjudicator can either be named in the contract documents at the outset, as in the JCT 1980 version of the Nominated and Domestic Sub-Contracts, or be chosen once the dispute arises. The advantage of knowing an adjudicator from the outset is that he can respond immediately, which avoids possible arguments over who should be chosen. The disadvantage of naming an individual is the breadth of potential disputes.

Under the DOM/1 and NAM/1, disputes were limited to the contractor's right to set-off. By contrast, in all but the simplest construction contracts, issues could encompass, among others, engineering, surveying, chemistry, architecture and the law. It should be remembered, however, that in certain forms of contract, particularly the ICE Conditions of Contract, Sixth Edition (1991), the engineer is called upon to exercise a similar sort of role under cl 66, which states:

---

1     Section 108 is set out in Appendix 1.
2     Scheme for Construction Contracts (England and Wales) Regulations 1998, SI 1998/649.

'If a dispute of any kind whatsoever arises between the employer and the contractor in connection with or arising out of the contract or the carrying out of the works including any dispute as to any decision, opinion, instruction or valuation of the engineer . . . shall be settled by the engineer.'

There is a similar provision in the Fédération Internationale des Ingénieurs-Conseils (FIDEC) Fourth Edition (the Red Book) in cl 67. The advantage an engineer has under these forms of contracts is that he is fully conversant with the progress of the contract, unlike an adjudicator who is simply called in when disputes arise.

While the final decision in a dispute must remain with the adjudicator, he may take advice from a specialist in a particular field. Some of the schemes drafted as alternatives to the Scheme for Construction Contracts expressly enable the adjudicator to take advice from specialist consultants. The 1996 Act does not expressly stipulate that the adjudicator should be a natural person (although the Scheme does so specify). It would be possible to nominate a multi-disciplinary partnership which could then supply an adjudicator at very short notice suited to the dispute. The major problem is the time constraint, ie whether the adjudicator named in the contract will actually be available to deal with the adjudication at short notice. It often happens in arbitrations that when parties do manage to agree upon the identity of an arbitrator, that arbitrator is not immediately available. This is especially likely to be the case if the adjudicator is in great demand. If he is available and the issues raised are not within his area of competence, the issue will be whether he has sufficient time to obtain specialist advice. Presumably he can do so only when he knows the details of the issues from both parties. If an adjudicator is named, he is named not only for that dispute but also for any subsequent disputes. This has the advantage of creating a consistency of approach, particularly if the same adjudicator is named both in the main and sub-contracts and possibly also in the consultant's appointment.

The alternative to nominating an individual or firm in the contract is to leave the choice of an adjudicator to a nominating body such as the Royal Institute of British Architects (RIBA), the Institution of Civil Engineers (ICE), the Royal Institution of Chartered Surveyors (RICS) and the Chartered Institute of Arbitrators (CIArb). A list of bodies which hold themselves out as being capable of appointing adjudicators is set out in Appendix 4. All such bodies should be capable of nominating an adjudicator within the seven days stipulated in the 1996 Act.

### 3.1.3   The timetable for the decision – s 108(2)(c)

The contract must require the adjudicator to reach a decision within 28 days of referral of the dispute, or such longer period as is agreed by the parties after the dispute has been referred to him. The time to reach a decision is relatively short – 28 days is typically the time allowed in an arbitration for a claimant to produce his points of claim (upon which he may have been working for some time prior to the directions given by an arbitrator at a preliminary hearing). It is clear that an adjudicator cannot comply with such a timetable (even if it is vastly truncated), particularly if he is to allow himself some time for reflection before delivering his decision. The 28-day period can be extended only after the dispute has been referred (to the adjudicator) by the agreement of both parties. It is not possible for the parties to agree in their contract for a longer period.

### 3.1.4 Extending the timetable for the decision – s 108(2)(d)

The contract must allow the adjudicator to extend the period of 28 days by up to 14 days with the consent of the party by whom the dispute was referred. This enables the adjudicator to extend the period only with the agreement of the claimant who has referred the dispute to him. Ironically, the claimant is more likely to have enough time available to him to compile his arguments and evidence before referring the matter to adjudication and, therefore, has less need for an extension. The respondent, on the other hand, may be less prepared; indeed, the referral of a dispute to adjudication may come as a surprise to him. It is possible that if the respondent is aware that the claimant is about to refer the matter to adjudication, either by applying to the named arbitrator or to a nominating body, he should himself consider making the referral. In this way, he becomes the referring party with the right to ask the adjudicator for a 14-day extension to the timetable.

### 3.1.5 The duty to act impartially – s 108(2)(e)

The contract must impose a duty on the adjudicator to act impartially. The *Shorter Oxford English Dictionary* definition of impartiality is 'the quality of being impartial, freedom from prejudice or bias, fairness, impartial is not favouring one more than the other, unprejudiced, unbiased, fair, just, equitable'. If it is accepted therefore that being impartial is the same as being fair, the importance of impartiality is highlighted. In *Russell v Duke of Norfolk and Others*,[1] Lord Tucker stated that:

> 'the requirements of natural justice much depend on the circumstances of the case, the nature of the enquiry and the rules under which the enquiry is acting ... whatever standard is adopted one essential is that the person concerned should have a reasonable opportunity of presenting its case.'

This *dictum* has been quoted with approval in many subsequent decisions. As that case illustrates, however, the much broader concept of natural justice applied to the conduct of trials and arbitrations will not be applicable to adjudication.

In *Annie Fox and Others v PG Wellfair Ltd*,[2] an arbitrator was found guilty of misconduct for having relied on his own evidence or opinion rather than that of the parties. This was held to constitute a breach of the rules of natural justice. However, as the 1996 Act enables the adjudicator specifically to take the initiative in ascertaining the facts in the law (s 108(2)(f)) this is clearly not compatible with the rules applicable to judges and some (but not all) arbitrators. The ultimate test

---

1    [1949] 1 All ER 109.
2    [1981] 2 Lloyd's Rep 514.

of whether the adjudicator has acted fairly is to see whether he has complied with the procedure laid down by the contract or the scheme for adjudication which has been incorporated in the contract, or, if none has been agreed, with the Scheme. We will return to this point again when dealing with the enforcement of adjudicators' decisions in Chapter 5.

### 3.1.6   Ascertainment by the adjudicator of facts and law – s 108(2)(f)

The contract must enable the adjudicator to take the initiative in ascertaining the facts and the law. The adjudicator is not to be a judge or an arbitrator, or a passive recipient of information and evidence presented to him by the parties; the timetable for reaching a decision does not allow that sort of luxury. The adjudicator is expected to initiate his own enquiries, although the 1996 Act does not make this a positive duty, stating only that the adjudicator be able to do so. It is submitted, however, that, if the adjudicator undertakes an investigation of the facts and the law, the investigation must relate to the dispute referred to him, and not to what he thinks the dispute should be. Having conducted investigations, should the adjudicator communicate his findings to the parties? Since the adjudicator will usually have been appointed for his specialist knowedge in the area of dispute, the parties must anticipate that he will conduct his own inspection of, for example, the site or the disputed section of the work and come to his own conclusions. Whether the parties are notified of the details will depend upon whether the adjudicator is obliged to notify under a particular scheme, or chooses to do so. It is submitted that an exception to this may be when one party is taken by surprise. In *Thomas Borthwick (Glasgow) Ltd v Faure Fairclough Ltd,*[1] Donaldson J stated that:

> 'a trade arbitral tribunal is fully entitled to use its own knowledge of the trade, indeed the fact that it has this knowledge is one of the reasons why it exists and performs a most useful purpose. Experience however dictates that this knowledge shall never be used in such a way as to take a party by surprise.'

Trade arbitrations are a special category of arbitration in which the arbitrator is active in ascertaining the facts. In quality/condition arbitrations or 'look and sniff' arbitrations, which assess the quality of perishable goods such as a cocoa, rice or grain, the arbitrators examine the commodity in question without the parties being present and rely on their own skill and judgment in coming to a decision. Their role can be closely paralleled to that of an adjudicator.

### 3.1.7   The adjudicator's decision is binding – s 108(3)

The contract must provide that the decision of the adjudicator is binding until the dispute is finally determined by legal proceedings (or by arbitration if the contract so provides or the parties otherwise agree) or by agreement. The parties may agree to accept the decision of the adjudicator as finally determining the dispute.

---

1      [1968] 1 Lloyd's Rep 16.

The parties to the contract are bound by the adjudicator's decision in much the same way as the engineer's decision under cl 66 of the ICE Conditions of Contract, Sixth Edition. Clause 66(4) of the ICE Standard Forms states that the engineer's decision is final and binding unless the recommendation of a conciliator has been accepted by both sides or the decision is revised by an arbitrator. Similarly, if one party fails to comply with the adjudicator's decision he is prima facie in breach of contract. The immediate rights and remedies of the other party for this breach will depend upon the terms of the contract. However, the 1996 Act provides that if the adjudicator's decision is an award of money, breach of contract will give rise to the right to suspend work (once seven days' notice is given) by virtue of the payment provisions of the 1996 Act, which are dealt with in more detail in Chapter 5.

If the contract contains an arbitration clause, whether an arbitration can be commenced immediately or must follow the completion of the works will depend on the wording of the contract. Clearly, if there is no arbitration clause the review of the decision will be by the court. Previously, under the provisions of JCT DOM/1 and NSC/C of 1990 as discussed at **1.2**, a more restricted adjudication procedure required a notice of arbitration to be served at the same time as the notice of adjudication. The arbitrator, once appointed, had the power to vary or cancel the adjudicator's decision before issuing his final award.

The parties may accept the decision of the adjudicator as final and binding, either before the dispute has arisen by including this into the contract (eg as in the ICE for consultancy work in respect of domestic or small works) or by agreement after the dispute has arisen. If, for example, the parties adopt the Centre for Dispute Resolution (CEDR) rules, the party dissatisfied with the adjudicator's decision must serve upon the other party a notice of dissatisfaction within 60 days to avoid the adjudicator's decision becoming final.

### 3.1.8   Non-liability of the adjudicator – s 108(4)

The construction contract must provide that an adjudicator is not liable for anything done or omitted in the discharge or purported discharge of his functions as adjudicator, unless the act or omission is in bad faith. Any employee or agent of the adjudicator is similarly protected from liability. The wording of this section is the same as appears in s 29 of the Arbitration Act 1996. This section resolved what had been an area of uncertainty as to whether arbitrators were immune from suit by the parties to an arbitration. This immunity is derived in large measure from considerations of public policy; arbitrators, like judges, should be able to retain their independence and should not be subject to the rehearing of an arbitration, which allegations of negligence necessarily entail.

From the wording of s 108(4), it would appear that an adjudicator enjoys the same cloak of immunity. The adjudicator has of course to act. If he agrees to be appointed but then does nothing, he could face being sued, at least by the referring party. In practice, the scope of damage to be suffered should be limited. It should be quickly apparent to a referring party if an adjudicator is simply failing to do anything. Certain sets of rules, for example rule 8 of the TeCSA rules, envisage the adjudicator being swiftly replaced if the chairman of TeCSA considers that he is failing to act with efficient despatch.

In s 29(3) of the Arbitration Act 1996, there is specific reference to s 25, which deals with the resignation of an arbitrator. It makes clear that an arbitrator is not immune from the effects of his resignation, unless it is excluded or limited by his agreement with the parties, or the arbitrator makes application to the court for relief. The issue is, if an adjudicator were to resign and there was no issue of it being done in bad faith, is he protected by this section from claims by the parties to the adjudication? It may be that such resignations in such a short time-scale will be rare, and, if they do occur, another adjudicator can recommence, without the considerable waste of time and expense that occurs in arbitrations. Nevertheless, as the immunity conferred does not provide for resignations, it is to be assumed that the parties cannot claim for the resignation of an adjudicator. The construction contract is between the parties. As such, this provision must be included in the terms of the agreement between the parties, and the adjudicator will normally require this. Alternatively, exclusion from liability will be part of the rules under which the adjudication is conducted.

Immunity of the adjudicator from liability is in respect of the parties to the contract; it does not extend to third parties. For example, if an adjudicator decides that piles have been driven correctly by the contractor (contrary to the opinion of the employer's representative), and the building subsequently collapses causing injury and damage to third parties, the adjudicator could be held liable to those third parties if it can be shown that he was negligent in coming to his decision. The wording of s 108(4) mirrors almost exactly the wording of s 29 of the Arbitration Act 1996 which confers immunity on arbitrators.

What is bad faith? In *Melton Meads Securities v SIB*,[1] Lightman J stated that 'bad faith' has a variety of meanings in different contexts. Outside the field of administrative law, it has a moral connotation meaning either malice in the sense of personal spite or a desire to injure for improper reasons, or a knowledge of an absence of power to make the decision in question. Any party who seeks to allege bad faith against an adjudicator must have prima facie evidence to justify that allegation, otherwise he risks his claim being struck out by the courts.

## 3.2   EXAMPLES OF SCHEMES DRAFTED TO COMPLY WITH THE EIGHT CRITERIA IN SECTION 108

Shortly after the publication of the 1996 Act and its eight criteria, a number of bodies published sets of rules for adjudication procedure, some of which also included a form of agreement between the adjudicator and the parties to the

---

1     [1995] 3 All ER 880 at 889.

dispute. Some of these updated sets of procedure are reproduced in Appendix 3 and are: the Construction Industry Council (CIC) Model Adjudication Procedure; The Institution of Civil Engineering (ICE) Adjudication Procedure 1997; the Technology and Construction Solicitors Association (TeCSA) Adjudication Rules – 1999 Version 1.3; and the Centre for Dispute Resolution (CEDR) Rules for Adjudication. The Technology and Construction Solicitors Association (TeCSA) Adjudication Rules – 1999 Version 1.3, replace the previous Official Referees Solicitors Association (ORSA) Adjudication Rules – 1998 Version 1.2, as a result of the change of the name of the court from Official Referee (OR) to Technology and Construction Court (TCC). All these rules comply with the eight criteria of the 1996 Act, and can be incorporated into a construction contract by the inclusion of a simple clause along the following lines:

> 'If any dispute or difference should arise[1] under the contract either party may refer it to adjudication by serving on the other parties to the contract a Notice of Adjudication. The Notice shall set out the matters in dispute and the remedies sought. The Adjudication shall be conducted in accordance with [the CIC Model Adjudication Procedure/the ICE Adjudication Procedure 1997/the TeCSA Adjudication Rules 1999 version 1.3/the CEDR Rules of Adjudication] or any modification or amendment which is current at the time of the Notice of Adjudication.'

The rules attempt to clarify the perceived problems of the 1996 Act and the adjudication procedure as a whole. In summary these are:

- the appointment of an adjudicator in the short time scale provided and the terms upon which he is to act;
- how the adjudication is to be conducted;
- how the adjudicator is to reach a decision and, if so, what sort of decision that should be in the short space of time allowed and how it should be communicated to the parties;
- the issue of costs of both the adjudicator and, in certain instances, the parties;
- the enforcement of the award and whether certain defences are excluded;
- in subsequent adjudication, arbitration and court proceedings, the liability of the adjudicator to the parties and to others.

We shall examine in turn the four chosen schemes to see how they deal with the above-mentioned areas.

## 3.3 THE CIC MODEL ADJUDICATION PROCEDURE SECOND EDITION

### 3.3.1 Introduction

The CIC adjudication procedure contains a number of optional clauses in brackets. If they are to be excluded, deletion is required. The general principle of

---

1    If it is desired to widen the scope of the adjudication clause, the words 'in connection with' should be added. See discussion on this point at **4.1** below.

the rules is stated at the outset as being to reach 'a fair, rapid and inexpensive determination and this procedure should be interpreted accordingly'.

When giving notice to refer a dispute to adjudication, a party must stipulate the issues to be adjudicated upon and the remedy sought. This is referred either to the named adjudicator, who has two days to respond, or, if none is named or he is not available, to the nominating body cited in the contract; if none is specified, this is the CIC, in which case the request and notice should be accompanied by the appropriate fee (see Appendix 4 for the address and telephone number of the CIC).

### 3.3.2  Conduct of the adjudication

The party requesting adjudication is required to send the adjudicator and the other party a full statement of case, together with the evidence relied upon. Thereafter, the adjudicator has wide powers either to deal with the matter on paper or at a hearing. This includes opening up any decisions, certificates, directions or notices in relation to the contract. The adjudicator can meet the parties separately. The adjudicator may seek technical or legal advice at the cost of the parties upon prior notification and may use his own knowledge and experience.

### 3.3.3  The decision

The decision must be rendered within the timetable laid down by the 1996 Act. No reasons are required, but the adjudicator can be requested to clarify his decision upon payment of an initial fee. Since the adjudicator is not liable for anything done or omitted unless it is in bad faith, there is an optional clause which adds the words 'whether in negligence or otherwise'. It is submitted that this inclusion be maintained. In *Smith and Others v South Wales Switchgear*,[1] it was held that a clause which purports to confer exemption from liability in order to cover negligence should include the word 'negligence', or some synonym for negligence. Although the preceding wording taken from the 1996 Act should be sufficient to cover negligence, it does no harm to make this explicit.

### 3.3.4  Costs

The parties are jointly responsible for the adjudicator's costs, although he can direct one of the parties to pay for all the costs. If he fails to come to a decision before the decision is referred to a replacement adjudicator, no fees are due save for the fees for technical/legal advice. Each party is to bear its own costs and expenses incurred in the adjudication.

### 3.3.5  Enforcement

An optional clause precludes any party raising a right of set-off, counterclaim or abatement in connection with enforcement proceedings. The rules do not state

---

1    [1978] 1 All ER 18.

whether failure to honour the adjudicator's award is a breach of contract, although this may be a term of the contract itself, and of course gives rise to the right to suspend under the payment provisions. See Chapter 5.

### 3.3.6 Subsequent adjudication, arbitration and court proceedings

The adjudicator cannot subsequently be the arbitrator unless the parties agree, nor can he be called as a witness in subsequent proceedings. No issue decided by the adjudicator can be revisited by another adjudicator but his decision is not binding if the dispute is referred to arbitration or the courts where it can be reviewed as if no adjudication has taken place.

## 3.4  THE ICE ADJUDICATION PROCEDURE 1997

### 3.4.1  Introduction

The ICE adjudication procedure contains a general statement of principle very similar to that found in the CIC procedure.

### 3.4.2  The appointment

The notice of adjudication served by the party seeking adjudication upon the other party must contain details of the dispute and the remedy sought, and, in addition, the details and date of the contract. This additional requirement is useful as it enables an adjudicator to check whether the contract is covered by the 1996 Act and was entered into after 1 May 1998. An adjudicator has four days in which to state whether he will act, as opposed to only two days in the CIC procedure. Under both procedures the parties can agree alternative adjudicators. The ICE procedure provides that a requesting party can accompany his notice with details of one or more persons who have agreed to act, from which the other party may select one person within four days of the notice.

If, within a further three days, no appointment has been made, reference is made to the appointing body in the contract or, in default, to the ICE, which should be sent the request for appointment together with the appropriate fee. If the appointment is made by the ICE, the adjudicator is to be appointed on the terms of an adjudicator's agreement which is appended to the rules.

### 3.4.3  Conduct of the adjudication

The referring party is required, within two days of the appointment of the adjudicator, to send to the adjudicator the full statement of his case. Thereafter, the adjudicator has a similar wide discretion as to how the adjudication is to be conducted as under the CIC procedure. The adjudicator is specifically permitted to rely upon his own expert knowledge and experience, and may open up and review decisions, certificates, and valuations, and seek legal or technical advice provided he has first notified the parties and given them details of the specialist's advice. As with the CIC procedure, the adjudicator must determine the matters set out in the notice unless the parties agree to add further matters. The ICE procedure does not specify whether the adjudicator may meet the parties separately.

### 3.4.4   The decision

There is no requirement or provision for the adjudicator to give reasons for his decision, but he can correct ambiguities or clerical errors on his own initiative or at the request of the parties within 14 days of the notification of his decision. Decisions on different issues can be communicated at different times. The adjudicator may also offer to deliver his decision up to seven days before it is due under the timetable laid down by the 1996 Act on payment of his fees and expenses. As with the CIC procedure, the adjudicator's decision may not be referred to a subsequent adjudicator, but can be reviewed in subsequent court proceedings or arbitration.

### 3.4.5   Costs

The parties are jointly responsible for the adjudicator's fees unless he fails to render a decision before the matter is referred to a replacement adjudicator. The parties remain responsible for any legal and technical advice sought by the adjudicator subject to their having been notified of the advice. This provision envisages such things as tests, the results of which are then communicated to the parties. The adjudicator may direct that his fees and expenses be paid in all or in part by one of the parties. If he makes no such direction, the parties pay in equal shares. The parties are to bear their own costs and expenses incurred in the arbitration.

### 3.4.6   Enforcement

There is no mention of excluding set-off or abatement when enforcement is sought. The procedure does, however, state that summary enforcement may be sought, regardless of whether the dispute is to be referred to legal proceedings or arbitration.

### 3.4.7   Subsequent adjudication, arbitration and court proceedings

The adjudicator cannot subsequently be called as a witness. Neither the ICE nor the CIC procedure deals with the issue of those who supply technical advice or assistance to the adjudicator. They are not excluded as potential witnesses, and may be crucial if they have conducted tests or observations relating to the dispute.

The adjudicator must not subsequently be appointed as an arbitrator unless both parties agree. He is not liable to the parties for his decision unless it is rendered in bad faith. In addition, the parties are jointly liable to indemnify the adjudicator for any claims by third parties. The adjudicator's immunity from liability under the contract applies only to the parties to the contract, and not to others.

## 3.5 THE TeCSA ADJUDICATION RULES 1999 VERSION 1.3

### 3.5.1 Introduction

The ORSA Adjudication Rules 1998 were the first set of rules to be published following the passing of the 1996 Act and are different in form and content to the two preceding schemes. There is a similar principle which states that the purpose of the adjudication is to resolve disputes as rapidly and economically as possible.

The rules became the TeCSA Adjudication Rules in 1999 as a result of the change of the name of the court to the Technology and Construction Court.

Adjudication is initiated by a notice identifying the dispute in general terms. There is no appended adjudicator's agreement.

If the parties have not agreed on the identity of the arbitrator, or he has not confirmed his willingness to act within seven days, either party may apply to the chairman of ORSA to nominate an adjudicator. This may be contrasted to the two preceding schemes where the party seeking the adjudication makes the application.

The application must be accompanied by a copy of the contract or other evidence that the ORSA rules apply, the notice of adjudication and an appointment fee of £100. Where an adjudicator has already been appointed in relation to another dispute arising out of the contract, the chairman may appoint the same or a different person as an adjudicator.

### 3.5.2 Conduct of the arbitration

Rule 3 of the ORSA rules states that the date of referral of the dispute (from which the 28-day timetable runs) is the date on which the adjudicator confirms his acceptance. The timetable and procedure are established by the adjudicator. This specifically includes making use of his own specialist knowledge and meeting one party without the other party being present. The adjudicator must, however, ensure that any written submissions he receives are also available to the other party. Specialist advice may be obtained when at least one of the parties either requests or consents to it.

### 3.5.3 The decision

As under the two previous schemes, the adjudicator has the power to open up any certificates or other documents issued under the contract. Significantly, the rules recognise that within the time available it may not be possible to undertake the necessary examination of the issues to arrive at 'a concluded view upon the legal entitlement of the parties'. The adjudicator is permitted to make a decision which represents 'his fair and reasonable view in the light of the facts and the law insofar as they have been ascertained by the adjudicator, of how the disputed matter should lie until resolved by litigation or arbitration'. The drafters of the TeCSA rules were concerned to tackle in the rules the issue of potentially complicated disputes being resolved within 28 days. This provision was drafted to enable adjudicators to come to a decision despite not having time for a full analysis usually available to a judge or arbitrator. The other procedures are less explicit upon this point; however, both recognise that it is not an arbitration nor a final determination in legal proceedings. The CIC rules, for example, expressly state that adjudication is neither arbitration nor an expert determination. The decision will not include reasons and there is no provision for requesting them.

### 3.5.4 Costs

Unlike the other schemes the adjudicator's fees are capped at £1,000 per day. The adjudicator is not allowed to request security for his fees, nor advance payment. The parties are jointly responsible for the adjudicator's fees except where it transpires that the party who requested adjudication had no right to do so, in which case that party becomes responsible for the adjudicator's fees. As with the other schemes the adjudicator may direct in his decision who shall be primarily responsible for his fees but, if no such direction is made, fees are payable in equal shares. There is no provision to order one party to pay the other party's costs; indeed, the adjudicator is expressly constrained from awarding legal costs.

### 3.5.5 Enforcement

No party is entitled to raise any right of set-off, counterclaim or abatement in connection with any enforcement proceedings. As in the ICE conditions, the ORSA rules state that the parties shall be entitled to 'summary enforcement'. Whether this will be achievable, particularly where there is an arbitration clause, is an issue addressed in detail in Chapter 5.

### 3.5.6 Subsequent adjudication, arbitration and court proceedings

The adjudicator cannot be called as a witness or named as a party in subsequent proceedings. He is not liable for his decisions whether in negligence or otherwise, unless acting in bad faith. The rules envisage that a party to the adjudication may make an application to the court relating to the conduct of the adjudication. The rules require that such an application should be delayed until the decision has been rendered and complied with, with the exception only of applications in relation to bad faith.

## 3.6 THE CEDR RULES OF ADJUDICATION

### 3.6.1 Application for appointment of adjudicator

Either party to a dispute may apply to appoint an adjudicator. The Centre of Alternative Dispute Resolution (CEDR) produces a standard application form which requires details of the parties, copies of the relevant contract provisions, brief details of the dispute and the redress sought. The CEDR states that it will appoint an adjudicator within seven days and notify the parties. The parties are required to enter into a formal agreement with the CEDR, although before the agreement is signed the parties are bound by the CEDR rules. Referral is made on the date of the adjudicator's appointment, or his acceptance of an appointment (where he is named in the contract).

### 3.6.2 Conduct of the adjudication

As in the other schemes, the adjudicator is given a wide discretion on how to conduct the adjudication. He must, however, ensure that both parties are provided with statements of other parties or witnesses. The party seeking the adjudication must submit a concise statement of the issues, to which the other party has seven days to reply. In either case, they may be accompanied by pertinent documents. The adjudicator may request further documents which the parties are obliged to supply, and can obtain specialist advice, but only with the consent of both parties. The adjudicator is given an absolute discretion in coming to his decision subject only to impartiality and good faith. This encompasses a power to review and revise any decision made under the contract.

### 3.6.3 The decision

The adjudicator should aim to reach a decision within 14 days of referral, only three days after receiving the response under the standard directions timetable. The adjudicator has the option whether to give reasons. In any event, he must reach a decision within 28 days, which is extendable by agreement of both parties, or by 14 days with the agreement of the referring party alone.

As these rules are formulated by the CEDR, the opportunity to mediate is permitted at any time before the adjudicator makes a decision. The adjudicator does not act as the mediator. If mediation is conducted successfully, adjudication ends. During the course of mediation the parties may agree to suspend the adjudication.

The decision of the adjudicator is stated to be binding upon the parties, although there is no explicit exclusion of abatement, set-off or counterclaim being raised in opposition to enforcement. Significantly, however, the decision becomes final and binding unless one party serves a notice of dissatisfaction within 60 days of notice of the decision.

### 3.6.4    Costs

The parties are jointly and severally responsible for the costs of the CEDR, the adjudicator and any adviser that the adjudicator appoints. The adjudicator can exercise a lien on his decision until the costs are paid. The adjudicator can apportion liability for these costs and those of the CEDR and any adviser that he appoints.


## 3.7    DIFFERENCES BETWEEN THE SCHEMES

### 3.7.1    Requirement to give details

The four schemes are more marked by their similarities than their differences. This is understandable since their main aim is to comply with the eight criteria under the 1996 Act. However, there are some differences. The ICE, CIC and CEDR schemes automatically require the party claiming adjudication to detail his case at or shortly after the matter is referred to an adjudicator. The ORSA rules leave this to the discretion of the adjudicator. Given the short time span, making this an automatic requirement is probably preferable.

### 3.7.2    Reasons

The CIC rules require the adjudicator to give reasons for his decision. The other schemes do not. Indeed, the TeCSA scheme states that the decision 'shall not include reasons'.

Some commentators feel that a decision should always be accompanied by reasons, at least to show that the parties' contentions have been considered. Others consider that giving reasons merely provides a platform from which the adjudicator's decision can be attacked and enforcement denied.

Reasons should not be confused with a structured decision. If, for example, payment is sought for different issues, ie physical damage and loss and expense for delay, the decision should mirror the request as far as practicable. A third party (often an insurer) may be called to indemnify a paying party for one part but not all of an adjudicator's decision.

### 3.7.3    Costs

On the issue of costs, the ORSA rules make provisions for circumstances where an adjudication is commenced at the request of a party who did not have an entitlement to adjudication. The issue is not covered in the CIC or CEDR rules. Presumably, these institutions will initially check the contract to ensure that the adjudication can be pursued. Alternatively, the adjudicator whom the parties agree to appoint will rule who is to pay. The TeCSA rules embody the maximum fees of the adjudicator per day. The CEDR scheme sets out the fees of the adjudicator in the adjudicator's agreement. The other schemes leave blank the hourly charge to be fixed by the adjudicator with the parties. This may provide an opportunity to a reluctant respondent to dispute the proposed hourly/daily charge, particularly if it is disproportionate to the amount in dispute. All the rules, except for the CEDR rules, deal expressly with the issue of legal costs. In each, the parties have to bear their own costs, which presumably includes, for the applicant, the nomination fee paid to the nominating body. The CEDR rules do not directly address the issue of whether the adjudicator can direct that one party pays the other side's legal costs. They do, however, enable the adjudicator to order that the winning party may recover from the other party any expenses incurred with the CEDR, which will include the nomination fee. They are the only one of the four sets of rules which expressly permit the adjudicator to exercise a lien over his decision until his fees are paid. The TeCSA rules expressly prohibit the adjudicator from doing this.

### 3.7.4 Set-off, counterclaim and abatement

The exclusion of defences of set-off, counterclaim or abatement in the TeCSA rules originated in the concern that the enforcement of adjudicator's decisions could be resisted by using set-off or counterclaim or abatement as arguments.

In *Enco Civil Engineering Ltd v Zeus International Development Ltd*,[1] although a certain sum of money had been certified as due, the employer had challenged this certification employing the machinery under the contract. The judge ruled that he could not give judgment for a certified sum, when that sum might be replaced by another certified sum. Additionally, there was nothing in the contract to prevent cross-claims being raised at the enforcement stage. This concern has been greatly abated by the decision of *Macob Civil Engineering Ltd v Morrison Construction Ltd*.[2]

### 3.7.5 Disputes 'under the contract'

The ICE rules state in para 1.2 that the object of adjudication is to determine disputes arising under the contract. The CIC rules contain similar wording, with an option to add the words 'or in connection with'. The ORSA rules state simply that the scope of adjudication will include matters identified in the notice requiring adjudication. The CEDR rules include the words 'where parties to a contract have agreed to refer disputes to adjudication in accordance with these rules'. Section 108 of the 1996 Act, and the words 'disputes arising under the contract', were discussed in Chapter 2. Choosing the CIC or ORSA procedure widens the scope of disputes which can be referred to adjudication.

### 3.7.6 Interest

The granting of interest is dealt with explicitly in the CIC and ORSA rules, but not in the ICE or CEDR rules. Although adjudicators have wide powers under all the rules, an explicit power in respect of interest on sums due may be preferable.

---

1    (1992) 56 BLR 43.
2    (1999) 96(10) LSG 28, (1999) *The Times* 11 March, [1999] CILL 1470.

## 3.8    THE SCHEME FOR CONSTRUCTION CONTRACTS

### 3.8.1    Application of the Scheme

Where the terms of a construction contract fail to comply with the eight criteria set out under the 1996 Act, or one of the schemes which does comply, for example the TeCSA, CIC, ICE or CEDR schemes, is not incorporated in the contract, the government Scheme for Construction Contracts will apply. The complete Scheme is reproduced in Appendix 1.

### 3.8.2    Referral of dispute

Paragraph 1 of the Schedule to the Scheme requires the party initiating adjudication (the referring party) to serve a notice of adjudication on every other party to the contract detailing the dispute which has arisen 'under the contract', where the dispute arose, the relief sought, and the names and addresses of the parties. It does not require the referring party to give details of the construction contract itself.

If an adjudicator is named in the contract, a request is sent to him together with a copy of the notice of adjudication. If no adjudicator has been named but a nominating body has been included in the contract, a request should be sent to that body together with a copy of the notice of adjudication. If the named adjudicator is unable or unwilling to act, application must be made to the nominating body. If no nominating body is stipulated, the application can be made to any adjudicator nominating body. A non-exhaustive list of these is set out in Appendix 4.

Prior to the final draft of the Scheme the government intended to have a list of approved appointing bodies, but has now abandoned that idea.

### 3.8.3    Notice to the nominating body

Whilst there is no requirement to supply details of the contract to the nominating body this may, nevertheless, be advisable. Many of these bodies also nominate arbitrators where it is commonplace to supply details of the contract and arbitration clause when submitting an application. This enables the body to check that adjudication is available, thereby reducing the risk that after an adjudication has begun and costs are incurred, the adjudicator subsequently determines that he has no jurisdiction because, for example, the contract was entered into before May 1998 or is with a residential occupier. However, nominating bodies do not act in the capacity of a court to determine whether or not the adjudicator has or will have jurisdiction. If the referring party insists on a nomination, the nominating body should not stand in his way.

### 3.8.4    Nomination

The nominating body can nominate individuals only, not firms or companies. The nomination must be communicated to the referring party within five days. Given the shortness of the period, most nominations will be communicated by fax or on the Internet. The person so nominated then has a further two days to indicate whether he is willing to act, but the nominating body should already have checked that this is the case. The ICE, for example, checks that the proposed adjudicator is willing and available.

### 3.8.5 Restrictions on nomination

The Scheme requires that the nominated person is not the employee of any of the parties to the dispute, and that person must declare any interest, financial or otherwise, relating to the dispute. While this precludes representatives of either parties, for example the employer and contractor, it does not, in principle, preclude, for example, the architect or engineer, provided he declares his interest. It may, however, be difficult for an architect or engineer acting as the supervising officer to discharge his duty to be impartial when the adjudication could concern a challenge to one of his earlier decisions. It would also be contrary to the ethos of adjudication which is meant to see an outsider to the contract acting as adjudicator.

Mustill and Boyd, in relation to the nomination of an arbitrator, state that it is a ground of objection that the nominee lacks impartiality 'in that he is closely associated with one of the parties, or with the subject matter of the dispute, as to cast doubt over his ability to conduct the reference judicially'.[1] Whilst an adjudicator does not have to act in all respects judicially, we submit that this analogy is a sound one. However, the internal rules of the nominating bodies may exclude this.

### 3.8.6 Failure to notify the parties

If the chosen nominating body fails to communicate the selection of an adjudicator within five days, the parties can either agree on an alternative adjudicator or make a request for an alternative nominating body. The same principle applies if the chosen or nominated adjudicator fails to respond within two days.

### 3.8.7 Referral notice

Once the adjudicator has been selected, and no later than seven days from the date of the notice of adjudication, a referral notice should be served on the adjudicator. This should be accompanied by copies of all documents upon which the referring party intends to rely. A copy of this notice, together with the documents, should be sent at the same time to any other parties to the dispute.

### 3.8.8 Further conduct of the adjudication

The adjudicator may take the initiative in ascertaining the facts and the law. He decides upon the procedure to be followed in the adjudication. He may request

---

1    Mustill and Boyd *Commercial Arbitration* 2nd edn (Butterworth Law, 1989).

any party to supply documents or statements in addition to those provided with a referral notice. The adjudicator can appoint expert advisers as long as he notifies the parties. He can make site visits with the necessary third party consents whether or not accompanied by the parties. He can also meet and question any of the parties to the contract and/or the representatives, and there is apparently no requirement that the other parties be present. He decides upon the language of the adjudication and can issue timetables and deadlines for the production of documents or submissions.

### 3.8.9    Failure to produce documents when requested or failure to comply with other directions

If one of the parties fails to produce documents or to comply with other directions, the adjudicator may draw such inferences from those failures as he feels are justified. When the documents or other information is communicated to the adjudicator after a particular deadline, he should attach such weight to that information as he thinks fit.

The adjudicator is required to make available to the parties the information which he intends to take into account in making his decision. This should include information he has obtained as a result of his own efforts. Where one of the parties has indicated that certain documents are confidential, the adjudicator or other parties to the dispute should not disclose them unless it is necessary for the purposes of the adjudication.

### 3.8.10    Oral hearings and representation

If the adjudicator orders an oral hearing, the parties can be represented by one person only unless the adjudicator directs otherwise. This condition is presumably aimed at parties who envisage coming to hearings with a battery of lawyers or consultants. If, for administrative reasons, more than one representative must be present, it is advisable to warn the adjudicator and the other parties why this is necessary so that the adjudicator can give his permission.

### 3.8.11    The adjudicator's decision

The adjudicator is charged with carrying out his duties impartially and in accordance with any relevant terms of the contract. He must reach his decision in accordance with the applicable law of the contract, avoiding all unnecessary expense. His decision must be made within 28 days of the referral notice (referred to at **3.8.7** above), unless the referring party agrees to extend the period by 14 days, or both parties agree to a longer period.

The adjudicator must decide on the matters in dispute and, in doing so, may take into account other matters which the parties agree should be within the scope of the adjudication, or which the adjudicator considers are necessarily connected with the dispute. The adjudicator has the power to reconsider any previous decision under the contract *unless* the contract states that the decision is final and conclusive. This exception was a late amendment to the Scheme. Whether or not a decision is final will depend upon the interpretation of the contract.

If the adjudicator gives no indication of the date by which his decision should be complied with, it is immediate upon delivery of his decision. The adjudicator can decide whether one of the parties is liable to make a payment. If, following the service of an effective notice of intention, he withholds payment served by one of the parties, the sum that the adjudicator directs must be paid within seven days of his decision.

### 3.8.12 Interest and reasons

Paragraph 22 of Pt I of the Schedule to the government Scheme requires the adjudicator to provide reasons for his decision if requested to do so by one of the parties. The adjudicator may prompt the parties by reference to this paragraph to see whether they wish him to give reasons. Such a request must, however, be made before he issues his decision. Once the decision is issued, the Scheme does not provide for any amendments. To permit parties to request reasons after the issue of the decision could mean such requests being made weeks, if not months, later. Put in another way, once the adjudicator has issued his decision there is in a way no longer a dispute.

The applicant seeking a monetary decision will no doubt also seek interest. In cases of small businesses seeking recovery from large businesses, that interest may be recoverable under the Commercial Debts (Interest) Act 1998 at a higher rate than may be provided for in the contract itself. Paragraph 20(c) of the government Scheme states that the adjudicator is to have 'regard to any term of the contract relating to the payment of interest'. This must mean that the adjudicator must bear the contractual provisions in mind, but he is not necessarily bound by them and can award interest when the contract does not mention interest, or set the rate of interest recoverable at a level which he deems to be appropriate.

### 3.8.13 Fees and costs

The parties are jointly responsible for the reasonable fees and expenses of the adjudicator. Even when the adjudicator has determined which party is to pay his fees, both parties remain ultimately liable. In the event that the adjudicator is not paid by the party who is ordered to pay (because he is insolvent), the winning party would have to pay his fees. Where an adjudicator ceases to act because the dispute is referred to another adjudicator, he is entitled to his reasonable fees and expenses. This also applies where he concludes that the dispute is different to that identified in the referral notice and he is not competent to act, or where his appointment is jointly revoked by the parties. The only exception to the adjudicator's right to payment of his fees is where revocation is due to the default or misconduct of the adjudicator, for example he simply fails to deal with the adjudication. In this case the parties are not liable to pay his fees.

The Scheme is silent as to whether the adjudicator has the power to award the successful party his legal costs. It is acknowledged that if both parties to the adjudication agree that the adjudicator has the power to order one side to pay the other side's legal costs, then he does have the power to do so. The parties have, in effect, vested the adjudicator with this power. Many commentators had interpreted the absence of any express power from the Scheme to award legal costs and expenses as meaning that the adjudicator did not have this power, not even to award to the successful applicant any nomination fee that they had paid.

In *John Cothliff Limited v Alan Build North West Limited*,[1] His Honour Judge Marshall Evans, a judge of the Technology and Construction Court in Liverpool, ruled that an adjudicator could award the winning party's legal costs under the government Scheme. The judge ruled that, in adjudications under the Scheme, a term should be implied that the adjudicator has the power to award costs 'as a necessary incident of a contract of this nature'. Whilst this decision stands, parties to an adjudication conducted under the Scheme should request payment of their costs of representation. This, of course, covers the cost of professional assistance in adjudication by lawyers or claims consultants or other experts. In *Piper Double Glazing Limited v David Caulfield*,[2] it was decided that an arbitrator could grant, and a court could tax, the costs of claims consultants. The same reasoning applies to adjudications. The parties should invite the adjudicator to indicate when they should submit to him the details of their costs. These should be submitted before he renders his substantive decision, otherwise there is a risk of his decision on costs being made after he has ceased to be the adjudicator and is *functus officio*. A useful template for the details to be provided in the statement of costs for the summary assessment can be found in the Civil Procedure Rules 1998[3] under the Practice Direction to Part 43.

### 3.8.14   Effect of decision and enforcement

The decision is binding upon the parties until finally determined by legal proceedings, arbitration or by agreement. The Scheme contains no express provision, precluding the pleading of set-off, abatement or counterclaim, but does state that s 42 of the Arbitration Act 1996 shall apply (with modifications). Section 42 is reproduced in Appendix 1.

### 3.8.15   Peremptory orders

Section 42 of the Arbitration Act 1996 is concerned with peremptory orders. A peremptory order is made in litigation, or, on occasion, in arbitration, usually when an existing order or direction has not been complied with. The order will usually direct that unless the order is complied with within a stipulated period of time, certain consequences will follow. For example, in court proceedings a court may direct that unless the defendant discloses certain documents that he was previously ordered to produce, within, say, seven days, his defence to the claim will be struck out and judgment may be entered against him. The Civil Procedure

---

1    (Unreported) 29 July 1999, TCC Liverpool.
2    64 BOR 32.
3    *Civil Court Service* (Jordans), p 1379.

Rules 1998, SI 1998/3132, which came into force on 26 April 1999 permit immediate use of peremptory orders.

Section 41 of the Arbitration Act 1996 gives power to an arbitrator to issue directions of such a type. This may ultimately mean, for example, that the claim is dismissed, or that an award is made against a respondent despite his non-appearance at an arbitral hearing.

A party to an arbitration may apply to court to compel conformance with a peremptory order which has already been made by the arbitrator but which has not been complied with. The parties have to agree that the court shall have this power. A court can make orders which an arbitrator cannot; for example a party can be committed to prison for failing to comply with the court order.

The Scheme provides that the adjudicator may make all or part of his decision peremptory. This suggests that his decision at the end of 28 days or longer, if extended, should be expressed as a peremptory order unless it is clear that his decision will be complied with. The decision must include the word 'peremptory'; for example 'By way of peremptory decision the Respondent shall pay the Claimant £25,000 plus £3,700 interest being a total of £28,700 on or before 1st June'. Unlike peremptory orders in court proceedings or arbitration, the adjudicator's decision cannot state what sanction will be imposed for failing to comply since this is beyond his jurisdiction. He cannot, for example, strike out the respondent's defence, or the claimant's claim as he has, in effect, rendered his decision on the matters in dispute.

### 3.8.16 Application to court for a peremptory order

Adopting the modifications made by the Scheme to s 42 of the Arbitration Act 1996 which change references to 'arbitral tribunal' to 'adjudicator', removes the necessity for the parties to agree that the court should have the power to make peremptory orders, and recognises that the adjudicator's decision is, in effect, finals. The procedure for applying to the court for a peremptory order is as follows.

- The adjudicator renders his decision, which is expressed to be peremptory and, preferably, which gives a date by which it should be complied with. That date should not be too close to the date of the decision otherwise it may provide a defence to non-compliance.
- The party in whose favour the decision is made, for example the claimant, ensures that the other party, the respondent, has received this decision.
- Where the respondent fails to comply with the decision by the due date, the claimant can seek the permission of the adjudicator that an application to the court for a peremptory order is made, at the same time giving notice of this request to the respondent and any other party to the adjudication.
- Armed with a copy of the original peremptory decision, the written permission of the adjudicator, and evidence that the respondent has received both the original decision and the subsequent requests for permission to

apply to the court, an application for a peremptory order can be made. The most appropriate division of the High Court for such an application is the Technology and Construction Court, either in London, or to a judge nominated to deal with Technology and Construction Business elsewhere in the country.

As discussed in Chapter 5 on enforcement, the courts are likely to be more willing to grant peremptory orders in relation to payments of money, rather than technical decisions of the adjudicator. Before applying for a peremptory order, other remedies, such as the right to suspend work for non-payment, should be considered. Where, however, this type of sanction is no longer effective (because works have been completed) an application for a peremptory order may be more appropriate. In such circumstances the application may be countered by many of the defences discussed in Chapter 5.

## 3.9   UTILISING DISPUTE BOARDS WITHIN DOMESTIC CONTRACTS

As explained in **3.8.4** above, under the Scheme the adjudicator must be an individual. Consequently, the appointment of a board of two, three or more persons would be contrary to the Scheme and invalid. However, the Scheme requirement that adjudicators must be individuals is not compulsory for a construction contract which is exempt from the Scheme. Accordingly, for construction contracts outside the provisions of the Scheme, the establishment of a dispute board (of any number of persons) is entirely a matter for the parties. Dispute boards are discussed in some detail in Chapter 6. For present purposes, it is worth mentioning that the government has introduced dispute-resolution panels for many of its major road and rail projects. Furthermore, the government has elected to establish dispute boards in contracts under the private finance initiative despite such contracts being expressly exempt from the operation of the 1996 Act. It may be concluded that the government recognises that the Scheme is more applicable for small contracts where the higher costs of a dispute board cannot be justified (and where regular visits to the construction site, a feature of dispute boards, are considered less necessary).

Domestic adjudication utilising a dispute board can be very similar in practice to 'individual' adjudications. The main difference is the closer involvement of the members of the board during the construction period and, understandably, the board's greater familiarity with the project, potential disputes and the personalities of those involved in the construction process. A board is thus better able to act quickly and grasp the core issues in any dispute. The strong similarities between the roles of an engineer and a dispute board are irresistible, except for the perceived partiality which stigmatised the role of the engineer (and which gave rise to the development of adjudication).

Each member of the board will participate in every dispute unless an 'adjudication board' is selected for each dispute from a larger panel or group. Although unusual, this arrangement may be practical on very large and technically varied projects, particularly those with multiple main contracts, for example the new Hong Kong International Airport (constructed between 1994 and 1998) and the Channel Tunnel. In the UK, at least three projects (two commencing following the 1996 Act) are known to have established dispute boards to adjudicate disputes which may arise between the promoter (government or private) and the concessionaire. In one project, the dispute board is also empowered to adjudicate disputes arising between the concessionaire and the works contractors. As concession contracts may last for many years, there is potential for the board to exist over or long periods. A European project, currently in the planning stages, proposes to incorporate a dispute board to function throughout the concession period of between 35 and 50 years. Presumably, the members of the board will be replaced from time to time.

Other variants include several boards operating on the same project but each with a different specialisation. For example, a technical board may deal with engineering and constructional disputes, and a financial board may deal with disputes of a purely financial nature. Consistency can be achieved by having the same person chair the various boards.

In some cases, an adjudication decision may be the majority decision of the panel. In other words, a dissenting view does not prevent there being an enforceable decision. In practice, however, it has been seen that the vast majority of dispute board decisions are unanimous. In at least one UK dispute board (which is compliant with the 1996 Act), a condition precedent for a party to serve notice of arbitration is that the dispute board decision is not unanimous.

# Chapter 4

## THE PROCESS OF ADJUDICATION

### 4.1 INITIATING AN ADJUDICATION

Where a dispute arises between the parties to a construction contract and the contract does not provide for adjudication of disputes, either party may refer the dispute to adjudication under the Housing Grants, Construction and Regeneration Act 1996 (the 1996 Act). In these circumstances, the following checklist might be appropriate to determine whether the 1996 Act applies.

– Is the construction contract and agreement in writing which falls within the wide definition of construction contracts contained in the 1996 Act (and described in Chapter 2)?
– If the construction contract falls within that definition, does it concern construction operations in England and Wales (in Northern Ireland and Scotland similar provisions apply)?
– If so, is the contract nevertheless excluded from the scope of the 1996 Act? For example, is one of the parties a residential occupier or is the contract for the installation of machinery where the primary activity is the processing of chemicals? If not excluded, the 1996 Act will apply.
– Does the dispute relate to what is stated under the contract to be a final or conclusive certificate or decision? Disputes over such certificates are excluded if the government Scheme applies.[1]
– Was the construction contract entered into after 1 May 1998? The key words are 'entered into', not 'signed'. It often happens that construction contracts, whether they are building contracts or consultants' appointments, are signed some time after the actual agreement is entered into. For there to be an agreement, there has to be consideration and an intention to create legal relations. Whether there is an agreement will be a question of fact. If what is to be done, and how much is to be paid are settled, there is, in most cases, a contract which has been entered into, even if the formal contract may be signed later.
– Is this a dispute or difference under the contract? The inclusion of the word 'difference' as well as the word 'dispute' confers a wider jurisdiction on the adjudicator. In *F & G Sykes v Fine Fare Foods Ltd*,[2] an earlier case, *May & Butcher Ltd v The King*,[3] was cited with approval to the effect that 'a failure

---

1    Scheme for Construction Contracts (England and Wales) Regulations 1998, Sch, Pt I, para 20(a); see Appendix 1.
2    [1967] 1 Lloyd's Rep 53.
3    [1934] 2 KB 17 (note).

to agree is a very different thing from a dispute'. The contract in question may require the parties to agree on certain things, ie something which they have left unresolved when the contract was formed. The 1996 Act makes it clear that the adjudicator can be called in to settle such a disagreement.

The words 'under the contract' confer a narrower scope than, for example, the arbitration clause found in the standard form JCT contract which contains the following words 'any matter or thing of whatsoever nature arising thereunder or in connection therewith'. For example, the issue of misrepresentation as to whether or not there was a contract at all would fall outside the scope of the adjudicator's powers.

The adjudicator has jurisdiction to deal with disputes arising under the contract, which includes arguments of abatement or set-off raised by the other party to the dispute in relation to payments of money. An adjudicator (as with an arbitrator) cannot consider counterclaims or cross-actions which lie outside the contract. The respondent to an adjudication cannot argue 'I have not paid you because you owe me money on another contract' since this is not something which arises under the contract and the adjudicator must disregard it. However, such a defence could be raised if enforcement of the adjudicator's decision is sought in the courts, since parties are permitted to raise as a defence cross-claims arising on other contracts, although this has yet to be tested in the context of the enforcement of an adjudicator's award.

## 4.2   THE TIMING OF A REFERRAL

We saw in Chapter 3 that a party to a construction contract has the right to refer a dispute to adjudication 'at any time'. The problem with this provision is that certain bodies in their standard form contracts have long-established methods of dealing with disputes which they have been reluctant to abandon. The ICE form of contract is an example. In the amendments both to the Fifth and Sixth Editions of the ICE Conditions of Contract, to make them comply with the 1996 Act, the initiation of adjudication is effectively postponed until a decision is rendered by the engineer under the contract pursuant to cl 66. A dispute is referred to as 'a matter of dissatisfaction'. If the engineer's decision under cl 66 is unacceptable or is not implemented, then, and only then, can an adjudication be commenced.

Arguably, this amendment to the ICE Conditions of Contract Fifth and Sixth Editions, and similar provisions in the ICE Minor Works Second Edition, and the ICE Design and Construct Conditions of Contract 1992 are against the spirit of the 1996 Act which permits a referral of disputes to an adjudicator 'at any time'. However, in practical terms, except in exceptional cases, is the challenge to the operation of cl 66 before adjudication worthwhile? The engineer or the employee's representative under the ICE Design and Construct Conditions of Contract must render his decision within 28 days of the matter of dissatisfaction being referred to him. The engineer does so in the knowledge that his decision can be submitted to an adjudicator immediately; a powerful incentive, it is submitted, to make the right decision. The engineer is already conversant with the operation of the contract, unlike an adjudicator who comes to the dispute knowing little of the background. Nor does an engineer require additional fees, as would an adjudicator.

The party initiating the adjudication may wish to consider whether to refer all or only some of the dispute to the adjudicator. Take, for example, a dispute about the determination of a contract. The contractor considers that the contract was wrongly determined by the employer, and he seeks a decision from the adjudicator to that effect. There is merit in referring this issue alone to the adjudicator. If the decision is favourable, he can then commence a second adjudication on the issue of what damages he is entitled to resulting from the wrongful determination.

This is completely contrary to what is done either in arbitration or litigation where all potential issues are made the subject of the proceedings from the outset. The short time-span of adjudication does not allow for preliminary issues which would allow for issues to be dealt with one at a time. Allowing the adjudication the full 28 days to concentrate on one issue will hopefully ensure that his decision will be properly considered. Not only is such a decision less likely to be challenged if enforcement is required, it could also mean that it is more acceptable to the losing party.

## 4.3 APPOINTMENT OF ADJUDICATOR

The 1996 Act provides that the contracts should secure the appointment of an adjudicator and refer the dispute to him within seven days.

If an adjudicator or a panel of adjudicators is named in the contract, the prior consent of the adjudicator to being so named will presumably have been sought and obtained. The adjudicator should, it is suggested, supply all the necessary details of how he can be contacted, for example his office address, telephone number, fax, e-mail and possibly mobile telephone number. The adjudicator should also indicate when he will not be available, for example because he is involved in an arbitration or court proceedings. This will at least alert the parties that they may have to employ a default mechanism and apply to a nominating body to supply them with an adjudicator.

The list of bodies which nominate adjudicators is set out in Appendix 4. Certain institutions are likely to nominate adjudicators from particular professions; for example, architects by the Royal Institute of British Architects (RIBA), engineers by the Institution of Civil Engineers (ICE) and lawyers by the Technology and Construction Solicitors Association (TeCSA). Other bodies draw their pool of adjudicators from a wider professional background, these include the Chartered Institute of Arbitrators (CIArb), the Academy of Construction Adjudicators, the

Chartered Institute of Building (CIOB) and the Centre for Alternative Dispute Resolution (CEDR). Most bodies require an initial fee ranging from £100 to £200 plus VAT. Some institutions set fees in advance, or cap the daily fees to their adjudicators, possibly by reference to the amount in dispute; others leave the issue of the amount of fees to be decided between the adjudicator and the parties. Details of this aspect are given in Appendix 4.

## 4.4   CONDUCT OF THE ADJUDICATION

The adjudicator must reach a decision within 28 days of referral of the dispute. As was indicated in Chapter 3, such a short period does not permit an adjudicator to follow the same procedure as in arbitration. The Scheme for Construction Contracts, the statutory code made under the 1996 Act,[1] suggests a number of powers the arbitrator may exercise, but these do not limit his discretion on how to conduct the arbitration. They include 'requesting parties to the contract to supply him with documents as he may reasonably require, including written statements, meeting the parties and all their representatives and questioning them, making site visits, carrying out tests and experiments and perhaps appointing his own expert or legal advisers'.

Certain disputes will be not be adjudicable in the time permitted. If possible, this should be recognised by the parties and the adjudicator rather than causing the parties to incur costs for either a non-decision or a poorly considered decision. Recognition of those disputes which should be 'dropped' immediately is not easy, and a robust adjudicator should call a meeting of the parties to advise them of his concerns and to seek further time if he is of the view that to proceed on the original timetable would be impracticable and wasteful. From anecdotal evidence, it appears that requests for extensions beyond the 28 days are emanating principally from adjudicators. Generally, these extensions are being granted by the applicants pursuant to s 108(2)(d) of the 1996 Act.

None of the rules governing the conduct of adjudication allow the parties to recover their legal costs. One or both of the parties conducting the adjudication may not be legally represented and the tribunal will need to ensure even-handedness and to prevent ambushes on the unwary. From experience with Dispute Review Boards, adjudicators in general are more approachable than arbitrators and they may be more willing to be proactive in searching out the truth and seeing a way through what might be a poorly presented (non-legal) submission. Adjudicators will generally be more willing to tell one of the parties during the course of the adjudication that they are 'pushing at an open door' to save that party deploying arguments in reply on an issue on which the adjudicator has already formed a favourable opinion.

The Scheme does not explicitly state whether the adjudicator will use his own knowledge and experience in coming to a decision; this omission is rectified in

---

1    Scheme for Construction Contracts (England and Wales) Regulations 1998, SI 1998/649.

some of the other sets of rules. It is the nature of adjudication that the adjudicator will, and will be expected to, use his expertise and experience in coming to a decision. It is suggested that as the object of the adjudication is to arrive at a decision which is acceptable to the parties, and, if not acceptable, which can ultimately be enforced without presenting too many grounds of challenge, the adjudicator in his inquisitorial role should ask himself the following questions.

– Do the specific rules which apply require him to obtain the consent of one or more of the parties before he appoints a specialist?
– When undertaking his own investigations or using his own knowledge or expertise, should he provide the parties with the information obtained and invite comment upon his preliminary conclusions based on his own experience before coming to his final decision?
– Should the adjudicator meet one of the parties in the absence of the other, and, if so, do the specific rules which apply permit this?
– Should the adjudicator extend the period under which he must come to a decision? He can do so by up to 14 days if he has the consent of the party by whom the dispute was referred.

## 4.5 REQUEST FOR EXTENSION OF TIME

As discussed in Chapter 3, it is more likely that the respondent will ask for more time to prepare his reply. Respondents in arbitration and defendants in court proceedings frequently request extensions of time in order to file a proper reply or defence on the basis that the plaintiff/claimant has had months in which to prepare before issuing the writ/notice of arbitration. If the respondent in adjudication genuinely needs more time, what should the adjudicator do when the claimant refuses to consent to an extension?

The first point to be made is that an adjudicator is not a passive recipient of documents from the parties. As described, he is to act in a proactive and inquisitorial manner seeking out information for himself. He is not dependent upon formalised points of claim and reply. If, despite this, the adjudicator considers that the respondent is labouring under a distinct disadvantage because of the lack of time available, he is entitled to draw such adverse conclusions as are proper from the claimant's refusal to grant the other party more time. It is suggested that the claimant be warned that the adjudicator may take this line to allow the claimant to reflect and grant the extension sought. A day can be important in an adjudication. Section 116 of the 1996 Act,[1] provides that, where an act is required to be done within a specified period after or from a specified date, the period begins immediately after that date. For example, the 28 days for a decision is calculated on the start of the day following the referral. If the dispute is referred to the adjudicator on 1 April, he has until 30 April to render his decision, or even a couple of days longer, if Easter intervenes.

---

1    Housing Grants, Construction and Regeneration Act 1996, see Appendix 1.

## 4.6   DUTY OF IMPARTIALITY

The 1996 Act provides that the contract shall impose a duty upon the adjudicator to act impartially. It is also important to be *seen* to be impartial, and relates to the choice of adjudicator almost as much as the conduct of the adjudication itself. The bodies which nominate adjudicators, and the adjudicators on their panels, will no doubt exclude from nomination those who may give the appearance of bias as well as those affected by actual bias. To this end, the appointing body, and the adjudicator whether he is named in the contract or nominated, should attempt to see himself through the eyes of the parties and ask 'even though I am fully satisfied that I can and will act impartially, could partiality be reasonably suspected of me?' An example from the field of international arbitration serves to illustrate this point. In *Kuwait Foreign Trading Contracting & Investment Co v Icori Estero SpA*,[1] the arbitration was being conducted in Paris. The chairman of the three-man arbitral panel was an English QC who happened to be from the same chambers as one of the advocates for the claimant. There was a challenge to the court by the respondents on the basis that the chairman was not independent from one of the parties. The challenge to the French courts ultimately failed but, on reflection, it is easy to see the basis of the application, even though there was no foundation for the allegation of lack of independence. The Organisation of Barristers Chambers in England and Wales, where every barrister is self-employed and where barristers from the same chambers frequently appear on opposite sides of the same litigation is peculiar to the UK. It is not therefore surprising that non-UK participants in an international arbitration should not necessarily be conversant with this practice and consequently have doubts about the impartiality of the tribunal.

The avoidance of the *appearance* of partiality should not be taken too far, however. The fact that an adjudicator has had previous commercial relations with one of the parties, or is known for his particular views on the regulation of the industry, should not disqualify him from acting as an adjudicator, although, preferably, any previous connections should be spelt out by the adjudicator at the outset.

## 4.7   THE ADJUDICATOR'S DECISION AND PAYMENT OF THE ADJUDICATOR'S FEES

The adjudicator is required to reach a decision within 28 days of the dispute being referred to him or such longer time period as is agreed between the parties. In some disputes the adjudicator will not need 28 days to reach a decision, while in other disputes making a decision within this time will be very difficult. The Act does not state, however, when communication of the decision should be made to the parties. However, para 19(3) of Pt I of the Schedule to the Scheme for

---

1     [1993] 3 ADRLJ 167.

Construction Contracts (the Scheme) requires the decision to be made known to the parties 'as soon as possible'. Some of the other schemes, for example the ICE Adjudication Procedure 1997, allow the adjudicator to make communication of his decision conditional upon payment of his fees, a device often used by arbitrators to ensure their prompt payment. The adjudicator can exercise this lien where the rules permit it. Where they do not, it is debatable whether such a right can be read into the requirement to reach a decision under such a timetable. The decision itself may have an immediate impact on the operation of the contract, and any delay could be detrimental. It is suggested that the adjudicator should exercise a lien over his decision only if the specific rules governing the adjudication allow him to do so.

Both the Scheme and the other adjudication rules provide that the parties are jointly liable to the adjudicator for his fees, although the adjudicator has wide discretion as to which party should be primarily responsible for the payment of fees.

## 4.8   GIVING REASONS IN THE DECISION

It has been suggested that the adjudicator should inform the parties of his reasoning during the course of the adjudication; whether he incorporates this reasoning within his decision is another matter. Some of the rules positively state that the decision shall not include reasons (the TeCSA Adjudication Rules 1999 Version 1.3). The Scheme states that reasons are to be provided if requested by one of the parties. The ICE Adjudication Procedure and the CEDR Rules for Adjudication are silent on the point, and the CIC Model Adjudication Procedure states that the adjudicator is required to give reasons unless the parties agree otherwise. The danger in providing formal reasons for a decision, when there is no requirement to do so, is that it gives the disappointed party an opportunity to show some default in the adjudicator's reasoning which can then be used to resist enforcement.

## 4.9   EFFECT OF PAST ADJUDICATION DECISIONS

It is possible that there will be more than one referral to an adjudication during the course of the contract. The 1996 Act states that the adjudicator's decisions are to be final and binding 'until finally determined by legal proceedings by arbitration ... or by agreement'. That much is clear. What is less clear is the effect of earlier decisions on later disputes, particularly when they are not submitted to the same adjudicator, or do not involve the same issue, even though similar facts may arise. In this respect, construction adjudication opens up potential problems which are not normally found in either arbitration or expert determination. In the majority of arbitrations, there is only one arbitration arising out of the contract, and one final award. The same is largely true of expert determinations. In construction adjudications, usually because the adjudication will take place while the contract is ongoing, there is the potential for a series of adjudication decisions. The Scheme provides that 'an adjudicator must resign where the dispute is the same or substantially the same as one which has previously been referred to adjudication and a decision has been taken in that adjudication'. This might be thought to be a reinforcement of the stipulation in the 1996 Act on the contractual binding nature of an adjudicator's decision. The case of *Ron Jones (Burton on Trent) Limited (Appellant) v John Stewart Hall and Jacqueline Dorothy Hall (Respondents)*[1] confirmed that the doctrine of res judicata and issue estoppel applied in consecutive arbitrations between the same parties where there were different arbitrators. The same principle must be true for adjudication.

The important thing, however, is to determine what exactly the adjudicator has decided in a previous adjudication. Take, for example, the previous decision upon an interim application for payment. The application contained an element for a variation. The contract provided for the revaluation of interim payments at the conclusion of the contract.

The employer served no statement of money due, nor did it serve any notice of withholding. The adjudicator decided that the amount that was applied for should be paid. Does this mean that the adjudicator has determined, definitively (at least as far as any future adjudications are concerned) the value of the variation?

Arguably the adjudicator has decided the value of the variation and this is binding in future adjudications, but much will depend on how the dispute is framed and the decision rendered by the adjudicator. If the dispute referred was simply for non-payment of an interim payment, and did not seek a valuation of the variation per se, then it would be possible for the adjudicator to award an amount for the interim application without having to determine precisely the value of that variation. For the avoidance of doubt, the adjudicator should make this clear in his decision.

However, what is the situation where a similar dispute arises, but the facts or evidence are substantially different? If, for example, the adjudicator has already ruled on a technical dispute but when a similar dispute arises the losing party to the first dispute has compelling new evidence to support his contentions, can the adjudicator hear this new dispute? In case of doubt, it may be better for an adjudicator to hear arguments on whether he is bound by a previous decision, rather than resign as directed by para 9(2) of Pt I of the Schedule to the Scheme. The other rules for adjudication do not contain a similar directive.

Does the Scheme refer only to decisions under the contract in dispute or to contracts between other parties? For example, if there has already been a decision in an adjudication between an employer and the main contractor, is that binding upon the same dispute between the contractor and sub-contractor? In principle, the judgment verdict or award of another tribunal is not admissible evidence to

---

1    Decision of His Honour Humphrey Lloyd QC, Technology and Construction Court, 7 April 1999, as yet unreported, available on Lawtel.

prove a fact in issue or a fact relevant to the issue in other proceedings between different parties (*Hollington v F Hewthorn & Co Ltd*[1]). Is this presumption (which is itself subject to statutory exceptions) excluded by the wording of the Scheme? It is submitted that it was not the intention of the subordinate legislation which introduced the Scheme to make adjudication decisions in one contract binding on another. Of course, the potential for conflicting decisions in the above-mentioned example would be greatly reduced if the same adjudicator were named both in the main and sub-contracts, although this would mean that the adjudicator would still have to hear the submissions and arguments of both parties in the second dispute.

## 4.10   ISSUES OF JURISDICTION

The respondent in the adjudication may challenge the jurisdiction of the adjudicator. Depending upon the contract and what has been referred to the adjudicator, there may be one or more grounds for such a challenge. Where the contract does not explicitly provide for adjudication, the following challenges could be raised.

–   Was it a contract entered into before 1 May 1998?
–   Is there a contract?
–   Where the contract involves work to a residential property, is the employer under the contract a residential occupier?
–   Is the sub-contractor who is bringing the claim not a sub-contractor but an employee of the contractor?
–   Is the contract for the supply of components only and therefore not a construction contract at all?
–   Does the contract fall within the list of exceptions given at **2.4**?

Alternatively, is the dispute which has been referred to the adjudicator one which arises under the contract?

The adjudicator can and should determine his own jurisdiction. One of the sets of rules, TeCSA Adjudication Rules, rule 7, specifically provides for this. However, issues of jurisdiction are much more likely to arise under the government Scheme where the parties have not drafted their contract to comply with the 1996 Act and presumably, therefore, have not addressed the issue as to whether this is a construction contract. Paragraph 13 of Pt I of the Schedule to the government Scheme enables the adjudicator to 'take the initiative in ascertaining the facts and the law necessary to determine the dispute'. This must encompass determining whether the adjudicator has jurisdiction.

Section 30 of the Arbitration Act 1996 enacted the internationally recognised doctrine of 'competenz competenz', whereby a tribunal can rule on its own jurisdiction. However, that ruling is not, in most circumstances, a power of final decision. It was made clear in *Project Consultancy Group v The Trustees of the*

---

1    [1943] 1 KB 587.

*Gray Trust*,[1] that a ruling by the adjudicator on his jurisdictional competence does not prevent a challenge to that jurisdiction being made if enforcement is sought. An exception would be when the parties had agreed to abide by the decision of the adjudicator on the issue of his jurisdiction. In fact, such a circumstance will be rare, as the party who objects to the decision of the adjudicator is likely to maintain that objection throughout the adjudication and participate in it under 'protest'.

Section 31(1) of the Arbitration Act 1996 requires a party to raise objections to the substantive jurisdiction of the tribunal at the outset of the proceedings. By analogy, in adjudication an objection of this nature should be raised straight away. If it is clear to the adjudicator that he does not have jurisdiction, it is submitted that he should issue his decision forthwith, if for no other reason than to avoid more time and expense being wasted by the parties.

---

1    (Unreported) (16 July 1999), TCC.

# Chapter 5

## EFFECT AND ENFORCEMENT OF ADJUDICATION

### 5.1 INTERIM DECISIONS

Section 108(3) of the Housing Grants, Construction and Regeneration Act 1996 (the 1996 Act) provides that the decision of the adjudicator shall be binding (until the dispute is finally determined by legal proceedings), by arbitration (if the contract provides for arbitration or the parties otherwise agree to arbitration) or by agreement. The parties may agree to accept the decision of the adjudicator as finally determining the dispute. When adjudication was first proposed as part of the 1996 Act, it was intended to be final and binding. Concerted pressure from the construction industry, however, changed that. One contract, the ICE Agreement for Consultancy Work in Respect of Domestic or Small Works, published in November 1997, does make adjudication final. As the name suggests, it is designed for small-scale consultancy work on behalf of householders and other small projects. An agreement with a householder would, of course, normally be excluded from the requirements of the 1996 Act, as described in Chapter 2.

Chapter 1 discussed the similarities and differences between adjudication, expert determination and arbitration. From an enforcement point of view, adjudication is closer to expert determination, although the majority of experts' decisions are final and not interim. An arbitrator's award enjoys a special status. Not only is it final and binding but if it is not honoured the award can be registered with the court by a relatively simple procedure which then turns it into a judgment. It can even be exported and registered as a judgment in many other countries by virtue of the New York Convention of 1958. It may be that under contracts where the term 'adjudication' is used, what is in fact meant is an agreement to arbitrate. This could be construed to be the case where the contract provides that the adjudicator's decision is to be final.

In *Cape Durasteel Ltd v Rosser & Russell's Building Services*,[1] the court held that the word 'adjudication' was not decisive either way to decide whether there was a binding agreement to arbitrate. It was a question of whether the agreement between the parties, in the particular circumstances of the case, did have the essential features of an agreement to arbitrate differences. The case was decided before the 1996 Act was enacted, although references were made during the course of argument to Sir Michael Latham's proposals on adjudication (see Chapter 1).

---

1    (1995) 46 Con LR 75.

Adjudicators' decisions do not enjoy the advantages of arbitral awards. For such a decision to be enforceable in the same way as a judgment, a court or an arbitral tribunal has to be persuaded to render a judgment on a decision that is interim and not final. This problem is illustrated by *Enco Civil Engineering Ltd v Zeus International Development Ltd.*[1]

Enco sought summary judgment on two unpaid certificates issued by the engineer under the ICE Conditions of Contract Fifth Edition. Before the writ, for some £163,000, was issued, the employer, Zeus, invoked the dispute procedure under the contract under cl 66 of the ICE standard form. Enco argued that until that dispute procedure had run its course the sums represented by the two certificates remained due and Enco should be entitled to summary judgment. The judge ruled that the engineer under the cl 66 procedure would have to rule on the employer's request for a revision of the two certificates. Even if no such machinery existed, it was clearly a bona fide dispute which gave the employer a defence and a possible cross-claim for damages. The summary judgment application was consequently dismissed.

There are few cases concerning the enforcement of decisions of construction and adjudications undertaken before the 1996 Act came into force. The first case to consider adjudication in the JCT family of sub-contracts was *A Cameron Ltd v John Mowlem & Co plc.*[2] The decision of the Court of Appeal was significant in two respects. It confirmed that an adjudication decision under DOM/1 was not an arbitration award (and could not, therefore, simply be enforced by registration). Secondly, it highlighted the important distinction between set-off and abatement. The sub-contract required the main contractor to detail its set-off against the sums that would otherwise have been due to the contractor. The adjudicator examined and rejected this claim set-off. However, in the absence of a provision to the contrary in the contract, the main contractor could still maintain a defence of abatement, ie an argument that the works had not been properly performed and therefore a right to payment either has not arisen, or at very least is substantially reduced. This confirmed an earlier decision in *Acsim (Southern) Ltd v Danish Contracting & Development Co Ltd.*[3]

In a subsequent case, *Drake & Skull Engineering Ltd v McLaughlin & Harvey plc,*[4] the adjudicator under a DOM/1 adjudication ordered that the contractor should pay a sum of money into a stakeholder account pending arbitration. The contractor failed to make that payment. The judge granted the requested injunction requiring payment to be made and dismissed the defendant's application to stay these proceedings for arbitration.

In granting the injunction, Bowsher J drew the distinction between a mandatory injunction which would anticipate the final outcome of the action, for example the knocking down of a wall, and the present case where the ordering of a payment of

---

1    (1991) 56 BLR 43.
2    (1990) 52 BLR 24, CA.
3    (1989) 47 BLR 55.
4    (1995) 60 BLR 102.

money into an account would be conditional upon the final outcome of the arbitration.

By granting the injunction, the judge also considered that he was enforcing an order made by the adjudicator 'in the course of the arbitration process'. In dismissing the defendant's application to have the action stayed for arbitration, he rejected the argument that the arbitrator could be asked to make an interim award stating 'that would defeat the whole purpose of the agreement which is to settle a particular matter'.

One of the major concerns of those who supported the introduction of adjudication clauses into construction contracts was whether the adjudicator's decision would be enforceable. There were concerns that the party in default would raise arguments of abatement or set-off or, alternatively, challenge the decision itself and those arguments would preclude the decision being summarily enforced. In addition, in contracts where there was an arbitration clause, the party ordered by the adjudicator would then say that the decision was disputed, and this could be resolved only by arbitration. This point is dealt with in more detail at **5.6**.

It was not until February 1999 that the enforcement of an adjudicator's decision came before the courts. In *Macob Civil Engineering Limited v Morrison Construction Limited*,[1] Macob, the groundwork sub-contractor, referred a dispute about non-payment of one of its applications for payment to adjudication. The decision in its favour amounted to some £300,000 plus VAT, interest and the fees of the adjudicator. Morrison did not pay, raising objections to the decision saying that it was in breach of natural justice and one week after the publication of the adjudicator's decision served a notice of arbitration 'arising out of or in connection with the adjudicator's decision'. When Macob issued proceedings in the Technology and Construction Court in London, Morrison issued an application to stay these proceedings for arbitration under s 9 of the Arbitration Act 1996.

It was agreed by both parties that the contract did not comply with s 108 of the 1996 Act, the provisions of which were examined at **1.3**; the government Scheme therefore applied. The parties were not agreed on the payment provisions in the contract, and this was one of the issues that had to be resolved by the adjudicator. Put briefly, one contract document stated that payment became finally due 15 days after becoming due, another document stated that payment was finally due after 13 days. The difference was crucial as Morrison argued that they had given notice of intention to withhold payment before the seven-day period specified in para 10 of Pt II of the Schedule to the Scheme.

The adjudicator held that Morrison's notice was not served in time and as a consequence payment was due.

---

1    (1996) 96 (10) LSG 28, (1999) *The Times* 11 March, [1999] CILL 1470.

Morrison raised a number of arguments. First, they challenged the merits of the decision. They then went on to say that the rules of natural justice had been breached in two respects:

(1) that the adjudicator should have given the parties an opportunity to make representations on the question as to whether an ambiguous payment mechanism was 'inadequate' as defined by the 1996 Act;

(2) that the adjudicator had made his peremptory order.

Because the contract contained a standard arbitration clause. Morrison argued that the court action should be stayed pursuant to s 9 of the Arbitration Act 1996, particularly in the light of *Halki Shipping Corporation v Sopex Oils Limited*.[1] That decision emphasised that a failure to pay could itself constitute a dispute which had to be referred to arbitration. Morrison emphasised that the validity of the decision was being challenged rather than its merits. This was to circumvent para 23(1) of Pt I of the Schedule to the Scheme which states that the adjudicator's decision is binding and enforceable pending the final resolution of the dispute by arbitration or otherwise.

Macob's argument, simply put, was that the decision was final, binding and enforceable until the challenge was finally determined.

In a robust decision which adopted a purposive interpretation of the 1996 Act and the reasons for the introduction of adjudication, the arguments as to the validity of the adjudicator's decision were dismissed. Dyson J drew an analogy with certain decisions of public bodies where a decision has to be complied with, unless or until it is set aside or quashed. He rejected the notion that a 'decision' whose validity was questioned was not a 'decision' that could nevertheless be enforced.

As to staying the dispute about the validity of the adjudicator's decision to arbitration, Dyson J ruled that the defendants could not have it both ways. It could not, on the one hand, say that the disputed decision could be referred to arbitration (as it had done by serving a notice of arbitration) and, on the other, argue before the courts that it was not a binding decision pending its revision. A person cannot blow 'hot and cold'.[2]

In concluding his judgment, Dyson J stated that, where it was sought to enforce the monetary decision of an adjudicator, an application for summary judgment was the most appropriate procedure.

Although Morrison had leave to appeal, that appeal was not proceeded with.

This first ruling on the enforcement of an adjudicator's decision was highly important in giving confidence to the procedures as a whole and to enforcement of adjudicators' decisions in particular. It also highlighted the importance of the payment provisions, the effect of which has been somewhat overshadowed by the adjudication provisions themselves. A paying party's failure to properly draft

---

1    [1998] 1 WLR 726, [1998] 1 Lloyd's Rep 465.
2    *Halsbury's Laws* 4th Edn, vol 16, paras 957–958.

those provisions and/or to fail to operate them properly by not serving notices within the proper time period, is likely to be fatal in defending a referral to adjudication by the party to be paid.

The decision also involved consideration of the government Scheme, which is likely to be widely applicable to perhaps a majority of construction contracts until, that is, knowledge of adjudication and the various alternative schemes become more widespread.

It was also important in answering the concern that the existence of an arbitration clause was a bar to rapid enforcement. Whilst it was argued at **5.6** that ideally arbitration clauses should be drafted so as to exclude application to enforce adjudicators' decision, there will continue, perhaps for some time, to be arbitration clauses in construction contracts without this exclusion.

If a construction contract is to comply with the adjudication provisions, it must contain a provision similar to s 108(3) of the 1996 Act:

> 'The contract shall provide that the decision of the adjudicator is binding until the dispute is finally determined by legal proceedings, by arbitration (if the contract provides for arbitration or the parties otherwise agree to arbitration) or by agreement.'

In this case, the contract did not include this provision, so the government Scheme applied, which essentially reproduced that wording. Stephen Furst QC, who represented Morrison in the above case, described it as a principle of 'temporary finality'. However it is described, the decision was certainly in line with the original aims of the Latham proposals and the spirit of the 1996 Act.

## 5.2 RIGHTS UNDER THE CONTRACT, SUSPENSION OF PERFORMANCE AND THE PAYMENT PROVISIONS

Sections 109–113 of the 1996 Act introduced a statutory framework for payment on all construction contracts. These provisions are derived from recommendations in Sir Michael Latham's Report, concerning unfair contract conditions.[1] Sir Michael considered that all parties should be encouraged to use standard form contracts without amendment, which should clearly set out and establish the timing of interim payments, deal explicitly with set-off and abatement and rule out 'pay when paid, clauses except in specific circumstances.

## 5.3 PAYMENT PROVISIONS (ss 109–113)

The same definitions of 'construction contracts' and 'construction operations' described in the paragraphs dealing with adjudication apply to this section. However, if a contract is specified to last less than 45 days, or the parties estimate

---

1 See Chapter 1 and Appendix 2.

that it will last less than 45 days, the majority of the payment provisions do not apply (s 109).

### 5.3.1　The importance and origin of the payment provisions

The provisions of the 1996 Act dealing with adjudication have received a substantial amount of attention, comment and criticism. By contrast, the payment provisions have received far less attention, yet the two are indissolubly linked. If adjudication is initiated, a majority of the claims will involve payment and whether the payment provisions have been complied with. Anecdotal evidence suggests that this has been the case in the majority of adjudications commenced since May 1998. This sort of dispute, ie whether or not the paying party is entitled to claim set-off, is ideally suited to the short time-scale of adjudication.

### 5.3.2　Adjudication/payment provisions; difference in application

As was seen in Chapter 3, if a construction contract does not comply with the eight criteria in their entirety, the government Scheme applies. The position on the payment provisions is slightly different. If one element is missing from the construction contract the relevant payment provision comes into play. For example, if a contract does not give the period for instalment payments, that period becomes 28 days. However, if the rest of the contractual terms on payment provision conform with the requirements of the 1996 Act, then they remain.

A party, contemplating adjudication because interim payments have been reduced or simply not paid at all, needs to consider whether:

– the payment provisions of the contract comply with the requirements of Pt II of the 1996 Act. If the contract does not comply either in whole or in part then the relevant provision, or perhaps all of the provisions in Pt II of the Schedule to the government Scheme, apply;

– the paying party has complied with the provisions of the contract. Where these are in compliance with the 1996 Act, and where those provisions are not in compliance with the 1996 Act, have they complied with the relevant provisions in Pt II of the Schedule to the government Scheme?

### 5.3.3　Periodic payments

Section 109(1) states that the parties to a construction contract are entitled to payments by instalments or other periodic payments for any work done. Under s 109(2), the parties are free to agree the amounts, intervals or circumstances in which payments become due. If they do not agree, the provisions contained in the government Scheme, made under the 1996 Act,[1] will apply (s 109(3)).

---

1　Scheme for Construction Contracts (England and Wales) Regulations 1998, SI 1998/649.

On the face of it, two parties to a construction contract can agree instalments, periods or milestones at whatever interval and this will ensure compliance. This could lead to contracts specifying periodic payments at four- to six-monthly intervals. Equally, instalment payments could be linked to completed stages of the works which may be achieved only two-thirds of the way through the project. However, whatever is agreed the contract must 'provide an adequate mechanism for determining what payments become due under the contract and when' (s 110(1)(a)).

### 5.3.4  Final payment dates

Section 110(1)(b) of the 1996 Act requires that all construction contracts provide a final date for payment in relation to any sum which becomes due. The parties are free to agree on what that should be, but, if they do not, the Scheme applies. It is open to the parties to agree that a certificate for payment be issued, but only finally payable in 40 or 60 days.

The term 'final date for payment' can be simply illustrated by reference to architects' certificates issued under the JCT Standard Forms. The contractor 'shall be entitled to payment therefore within 14 days from the date of issue of each Interim Certificate'. When the certificate is issued, payment is due; when 14 days has expired payment is finally due.

### 5.3.5  Set-off, abatements or deductions

Section 110(2) of the 1996 Act states that whatever periods are agreed for milestone, periodic or instalment payments, and the dates when they finally become due, every construction contract must provide that a notice be given within five days of the payment of the amount due to the payee if he had complied in every way with the contract and there were no sums due from the payee to the payer on this or any other contract. In other words, the statement should set out sums that would be due, and then show the deductions or abatements from that sum.

For example, if a main contractor considers that a sub-contractor has not done the work properly the reduction in the sum due must be clearly shown, as should any set-offs, contra charges or sums due on other contracts. If the contract does not provide for this, the Scheme applies.

### 5.3.6  Notice of intention to withhold payment

A party to a construction contract cannot withhold payment of part or all of a sum due under the contract after the final date for payment unless 'effective' notice has been given of an intention to withhold (s 111(1)).

### 5.3.7 What is an effective notice?

While notice may be given adequately in the form described at **5.3.5** above, s 111 requires that it must specify the amount proposed to be withheld and the ground or grounds for withholding it. If there is more than one ground, the notice must set out the sums attributable to each ground. Such notice must be given a prescribed period before the final date for payment, which can be of any length but, if none is agreed, the Scheme applies.

### 5.3.8 Effective notice – adjudication

Where a notice of set-off or reduction is effectively given (ie adequate information is given in sufficient time) and is then followed by an adjudication where the payer is required to pay, payment must be made within seven days, unless the original final date for payment (for that instalment) is more than seven days from the date of the adjudicator's decision, in which case that will be the date for final payment.

### 5.3.9 Right to suspend for non-payment (s 112)

Suspension of performance of the contract is one method of enforcement of an adjudicator's monetary decision which has not been honoured. Other circumstances where work can be suspended are where a sum due is not paid by the final date for payment and no *effective* notice to withhold payment has been given.

Once the time for serving an effective notice has passed, the paying party's only choice appears to be to pay, that is, if he wishes to avoid suspension and possibly an adjudication.

The defaulting party must give seven days' notice before suspending work, citing the ground for suspension. Suspension ceases once payment of the amount due is made. The 1996 Act does not state whether a payer's ineffective notice can be rectified, and refers only to payment being made.

The 1996 Act provides that periods of suspension are to be disregarded for the purpose of the contract period, contractual time-limits relating to the party suspending, or a third party who is directly or indirectly affected by the exercise of that right. The 1996 Act does not state whether the suspending party is entitled to claim for loss and expense, but, in principle, as the payer is in breach of contract this should be claimable. Amendment 18 to the JCT Standard Form of Contract provides that loss and expenses are recoverable by a contractor who suspends for non-payment, provided the suspension was not frivolous or vexatious.

Suspension does not mean termination. This would mean, so far as the contractor is concerned, that whilst he has no obligation to 'carry out and complete the works',[1] during the period of suspension he still has other obligations, such as insurance and securing the site.

---

1 JCT Standard Form, Private with Quantities, cl 2.1.

## 5.3.10   Prohibition of conditional payment provisions (s 113)

The aim of s 113 is to outlaw 'pay when paid' provisions. The only exception to such provisions is where the ultimate payer (usually the employer) becomes insolvent. For a company this means a winding-up order, but also includes an administration order. For partnerships, 'insolvency' is defined as occurring when a winding-up order is made, and for an individual 'insolvency' occurs when a bankruptcy order is made.

## 5.3.11   Instalment or periodic payments

Where the parties have failed to provide for instalment or periodic payments, or have failed in accordance with s 109(2) of the 1996 Act to agree the amounts of payments and their intervals and in what circumstances they became due, then Pt II of the government Scheme applies. Payment for the relevant period should be for the value of work executed during that period, together with materials brought onto site for the works, plus other sums which the contract specifies should be paid, less payments already paid or due for that work and/or materials. The relevant period may be specified in the contract but, if no period is provided, this is 28 days.

## 5.3.12   Dates for payment

If the contract is silent or unsatisfactory on when payment becomes due and/or payable, this will be either seven days after the relevant period, or the date when a claim is made for payment by a payee, whichever is later. That payment finally becomes due 17 days later.

## 5.3.13   Final payments

Final payment under the contract (defined as the balance after deduction of all instalment payments which have become due) is either 30 days following completion of the works or the making of a claim by the payee, whichever is later. Similarly, for contracts lasting less than 45 days (which are excluded from the other provisions relating to payment) the same principles apply. 'Completion' is not defined, but the wording suggests that final rather than practical completion is meant.

## 5.3.14   Notices of amount of payment

Notices of the amount of payment should state how much is due before listing the amounts by which it is to be reduced by way of abatement or set-off. The notice must be given within five days of the payment becoming due. If a notice of intention to withhold part or all of this payment is to be made, this must be given at least seven days before the date for final payment.

When calculating time both for adjudication and for the payment provisions, all days count (including Saturdays and Sundays) except bank holidays, Christmas Day and Good Friday.

Tables 1 and 2 below set out in diagrammatic form the time periods set out in the Scheme which apply when no equivalent time periods are stipulated in the contract.

## 5.3.15    Effect of payment provision on adjudication

The payment provisions in the 1996 Act do not go much further than the provisions that already exist in many standard form main and sub-contracts. They will, however, come into play when contracts are drafted unsatisfactorily or where no express terms dealing with periodic and final payments have been agreed. In adjudications concerning unpaid monies (which are likely to be the overwhelming majority of adjudications), payment provisions will provide the contractual blue print upon which the adjudicator can rule. Contracts drafted to comply with the 1996 Act, which thereby avoid the implementation of the Scheme, will no doubt deal with such issues as whether loss and expense is recoverable by a suspending party. They should also streamline the notice procedure, requiring of the payer one comprehensive notice setting out payments to date, and what is due, and when, if any, that amount is to be abated, reduced or eliminated by set-off.

A number of adjudications since May 1998 have had, as their major issue, whether or not an effective notice of intention to withhold payment has been served. See **5.3.6** and s 111(2) of the 1996 Act. If it is clear that no effective notice has been served then payment must be made. What is less clear is the position in relation to a failure to serve the earlier notice required by s 110(2) of the 1996 Act (see **5.3.5** above). Section 111(2) states that a notice of intention to withhold payment can effectively be constituted by notice under s 110(2). However, what is the position if no notice is served pursuant to s 110(2)? Is this a condition precedent for serving an effective notice under s 111(2), or is an effective notice pursuant to s 111(2) all that is necessary? The object of the earlier notice is to act as an indication of the value that the paying party puts upon the payee's application. In some construction contracts, this will be a process certification. If no such notice is served pursuant to s 110(2), does this mean that the payee is entitled to be paid the amount of his application for payment? One interpretation of the payment provisions would suggest that this is so, and, if a payment is not made (assuming no notice of set-off under s 111(2) within the requisite time period), then it is considered that an adjudicator is bound to decide that the amount that was applied for is due. Some adjudicators have, however, taken the view that they need to satisfy themselves that the value of the application actually reflects the work that was done. It is submitted that the failure to serve the notice under s 110(2) (the 'money due' statement) must mean that a heavy burden is placed on the paying party, who subsequently suggests that the application was excessive. Only when it is demonstrably the case that the original application was excessive,

*Table 1: Interim and/or Periodic Payments*

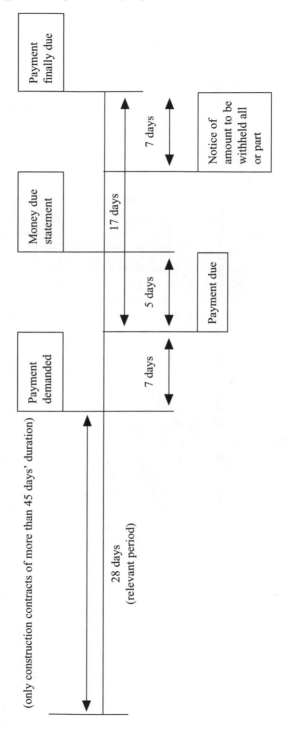

*Table 2: Final Payments on all Construction Contracts*

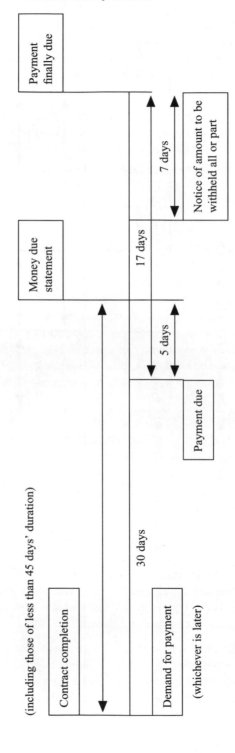

should the adjudicator consider not awarding the full amount of the application in his decision. One could envisage for example an application for the quasi totality of the contract sum when it is abundantly clear that nothing like that amount of work has been done and the contract does not provide for such an advance payment.

There may be circumstances where the right to suspend performance is ineffective, for example where by the time the adjudicator's decision has been made and the seven days' notice given, the contract works have come to an end. Alternatively, the adjudicator's decision may not be a monetary one. The right to suspend refers only to non-payment, not to non-compliance with the decision of an adjudicator.

## 5.4 APPLICATIONS TO THE COURT

The case of *Macob Civil Engineering Limited v Morrison Construction Limited*,[1] discussed at **5.1**, has greatly clarified what steps should be taken to enforce an adjudicator's monetary decision which remains unpaid. It has resolved some commentators' doubts as to whether arguments of set-off or abatement could be raised as a defence to enforcement proceedings. Dyson J stated that the most appropriate procedure for enforcing a monetary adjudication decision was an application for summary judgment, now governed by Pt 24 of the Civil Procedure Rules 1998 (CPR 1998).

The case of *Outwing Construction Limited v H. Randell & Sons Limited*[2] illustrates further that courts, in particular the Technology and Construction Court, are prepared to facilitate enforcement by means of summary judgment. In that case, his Honour Judge Humphrey Lloyd QC approved of the plaintiff's application to abridge time for filing an acknowledgement of service and serving an affidavit in reply to the application for summary judgment. This was justified, bearing in mind the strict timetable imposed by s 108 of the 1996 Act. Under the CPR 1998, the Court would now use its power pursuant to r 3.1(2)(a). In the case of *A & D Maintenance and Construction Limited v Pagehurst Construction Services Limited*,[3] an argument that the right to adjudicate a dispute under a construction contract ended when the contract was terminated was rejected. His Honour Judge Wilcox pointed out the analogy with arbitration clauses which survive the determination of the contract.

Cases under the 1996 Act have been few and have all dealt with a failure to honour a monetary adjudicator's decision. Some adjudication decisions, albeit a minority, will be non-monetary. The question remains: will the court be prepared to grant monetary injunctions in order to enforce non-monetary decisions?

---

1   1999 96(10) LSG 28, (1999) *The Times*, 11 March.
2   (1999) as yet unreported; available on Lawtel.
3   July 1999, Technology and Construction Court, as yet unreported; available on Lawtel.

Although the adjudicator's decision is expressed to be binding 'until finally determined by legal proceedings, by arbitration or by agreement', in effect certain decisions could be final. For example, a dispute arises where a contractor objects to a proposed nominated sub-contractor under the JCT standard form of building contract. The dispute is referred to the adjudicator who rules that the contractor's objections are valid. It is little comfort to the employer if the adjudicator's decision is reviewed and reversed in an arbitration some years later. Similarly, if an architect orders that a wall should be demolished because of an excess of mortar droppings in the cavities, and the adjudicator disagrees, stating that the walls should remain standing, where that decision is honoured, but is later overturned by an arbitrator or in court proceedings, it will be meaningless, since by then the building will be complete.

It must be emphasised that issus of enforcement arise only when the parties do not abide by the decision of the adjudicator. Evidence from dispute review boards suggest that, in general, such decisions are respected.

One of the reasons cited by the judge in *Drake & Skull v McLaughlin & Harvey plc*[1] for granting the injunction was that the injunction was conditional, and effective only until arbitration, rather than one which anticipated the final result of the action. In *Locabail Finance v Ager Export (The Seahawk)*,[2] Mustill LJ quoted with approval from *Halsbury's Laws of England*, 4th edn, on mandatory injunctions made in interlocutory applications, ie those not made at final trial when the judge has the opportunity to evaluate all the evidence. The passage reads:

> 'a mandatory injunction can be granted on an interlocutory application as well as at the hearing, but in the absence of special circumstances it will not normally be granted. However if the case is clear and one which the court thinks ought to be decided at once, or if the act done is a simple and summary one which can easily be remedied, or if the defendant attempts to steal on the march of the plaintiff . . . a mandatory injunction will be granted on an interlocutory application.'

After reviewing with approval *Shephard Homes Ltd v Sandham*,[3] Mustill LJ went on to say that an application for a mandatory injunction 'should be approached with caution and the relief granted only in a clear case'.

This reluctance to grant a mandatory injunction relating to an adjudicator's non-monetary decision may also extend to a decision where a sum of money has been awarded. Where the paying party can demonstrate that if the claimant is financially unstable and the adjudication decision, when reviewed ultimately by a court on arbitration, required it to be repaid, by which time the claimant would be unable to repay the money, in these circumstances, would a court nevertheless grant summary judgment? On the reasoning in *Macob Civil Engineering Limited v Morrison Construction Limited* (above), the principle of 'temporary finality'

---

1    (1995) 60 BLR 102.
2    [1986] 1 WLR 657, [1986] 1 Lloyd's Rep 317.
3    [1971] Ch 340.

would suggest that courts would not be impressed by this argument, particularly if it has already been raised and rejected by the adjudicator.

Adjudication was conceived as a speedy method of dealing with disputes over payment. A party seeking a decision from an adjudicator on a non-monetary issue should perhaps provide an alternative monetary remedy. In the above example of the wall, the contractor sought to reverse the decision of the architect that the wall should be demolished. In the alternative, if he must demolish the wall, he should be paid for its demolition and rebuilding. This is clearly a simple example, but it then puts the onus on the employer and his architect. If the architect is convinced that in his professional opinion the wall should come down, he will have to sustain this opinion before an arbitrator or a judge when the matter finally comes to be reviewed. Prior to the right to adjudicate, the contractor would have had to comply with the direction to demolish and would not have been paid for doing so. His remedy would have been to seek a review of the supervising officer's opinion in court proceedings or in arbitration. The position is now reversed. The money will be in the pocket of the contractor and the employer will have to seek its recovery.

## 5.5 DIFFERING OPINIONS BETWEEN THE ADJUDICATOR AND THE EMPLOYER'S PROFESSIONAL TEAM

If the adjudicator comes to a different conclusion on a non-monetary issue to that of the employer's professional advisers, what should those advisers do? Should they acquiesce on the adjudicator's decision and advise their clients to comply, or should they adhere to their previously expressed opinions and advise their client not to follow the adjudicator's decision and suffer the alternative financial consequences?

Again, such a situation is unusual. An adjudicator with appropriate professional qualifications will engage in his own investigations during the limited time available to him. He will discuss the matter with a professional adviser responsible for the original decision, and will be reluctant to reverse the decision on technical grounds without being sure that he has fully appraised the situation and is aware of all the considerations. If he does come to a different conclusion, he may persuade the consultant that the adjudicator's decision is equally acceptable. If, despite this, the employer's consultant remains convinced of his own earlier decision, he cannot expect to devolve his professional responsibility onto the adjudicator. If the adjudicator is ultimately proved to be wrong, the client will still hold the consultant responsible, unless there are clear contractual provisions which exclude his liability for decisions of the adjudicator. Given that the adjudicator is cloaked with a degree of immunity under the 1996 Act, which may be extended by the particular adjudication rules used, it is unlikely that the employer will agree to such restriction on the consultant's liability.

## 5.6   ARBITRATION CLAUSES IN CONSTRUCTION CONTRACTS

Where a contract contains an arbitration clause, the parties have agreed to refer all their disputes arising under, and often in connection with, the contract to arbitration. While the parties have the right under the 1996 Act to refer their immediate disputes to adjudication, what happens if that decision is not honoured and the party who has the benefit of the decision wishes to enforce it?

Prior to the Arbitration Act 1996, the courts retained a discretion not to stay court proceedings brought before them where there was an arbitration clause in contracts between nationals of England and Wales. That discretion was removed by the passing of the Act. Section 9(1) provides:

> 'A party to an arbitration agreement against whom legal proceedings are brought (whether by way of claim or counterclaim) in respect of a matter which under the agreement is to be referred to arbitration may (upon notice to the other parties to the proceedings) apply to the court in which the proceedings have been brought to stay the proceedings so far as they concern that matter.'

On an application under s 9, the court shall grant a stay unless satisfied that the arbitration agreement is null, void, inoperative or incapable of being performed.

Prior to the passing of the Arbitration Act 1996, applications were made to the courts for summary judgment, despite there being an arbitration clause in the contract in question. The argument advanced was that as there was no genuine dispute (summary judgment only being granted in the absence of a genuine dispute) there was no dispute to refer to arbitration. This approach relied, in part, upon s 1(1) of the Arbitration Act 1975 which stated:

> 'If any party to an arbitration agreement to which this section applies ... commences any legal proceedings in any court against any other party to the agreement ... in respect of any matter agreed to be referred, any party to the proceedings may ... apply to the court to stay the proceedings; and the court unless satisfied that ... there is not in fact any dispute between the parties with regard to the matter agreed to be referred shall make an order staying the proceedings.'

In *Halki Shipping Corporation v Sopex Oils Ltd*,[1] the plaintiff sought summary judgment for liquidated damages for delay. The defendants did not put in a defence to the claim, but nor did they admit it. The Court of Appeal held that in the absence of an admission to pay the sum claimed, s 9 of the Arbitration Act 1996 meant that there was a dispute which had to be referred to arbitration.

Nevertheless, this argument was raised and rejected in *Macob Civil Engineering Limited v Morrison Construction Limited*. To render the contractual position clear, and thereby reduce the scope to defer enforcement by the issue of a summons to stay, a modified form of arbitration clause is to be preferred.

---

1    [1988] 1 Lloyd's Rep 465.

## 5.7 MODIFYING THE ARBITRATION CLAUSE

A party to an arbitration agreement against whom legal proceedings are brought (whether by way of claim or counterclaim) in respect of a matter which, under the agreement, is to be referred to arbitration may (upon notice to the other parties to the proceedings) apply to the court in which the proceedings have been brought to stay the proceedings so far as they concern that matter. If a standard arbitration clause were to read 'if any dispute or difference as to the construction of this contract or any matter or thing of whatsoever nature arising thereunder, or in connection therewith *with the exception of steps taken to enforce or ensure compliance with an adjudicator's decision* ... shall be referred to arbitration',[1] the enforcement of an adjudicator's decision would be taken outside the scope of the arbitration clause. Amendment 18 to JCT 80 Standard Form of Contract now amends the arbitration clause to include the words 'except in connection with the enforcement of any decision of an adjudicator appointed to determine a dispute or difference arising thereunder'.

## 5.8 ENDOWING THE ARBITRATOR WITH THE POWER TO MAKE A PROVISIONAL AWARD: INTERIM AWARDS

Under s 39(1) of the Arbitration Act 1996 the parties to an arbitration agreement are free to agree that the 'tribunal shall have power to order on a provisional basis any relief which it would have power to grant in a final award'. This would enable an arbitrator to make a provisional order (as distinct from an interim award) on a temporary basis which could then be adjusted in the final award. An arbitrator may be persuaded to grant such an order if there is an indisputable sum due, even though the exact sum may require some adjustment. However, the arbitrator may be more reluctant if repayment of whole or part is likely to be difficult or impossible, due to the insolvency of the claimant. Further, the arbitrator is making an order, not an award. Enforcement by registration with the court under s 66 of the Arbitration Act 1996 is not available. An arbitrator does have the power to make interim awards (unless the parties remove that right) pursuant to s 47 of the Act. Interim awards, although made prior to the conclusion of the arbitral proceedings, are final as to the matters they determine. Such a procedure may enable an important issue to be decided early on, leaving the rest of the claim to be agreed upon between the parties. An interim award could also be sought where the adjudicator's monetary decision was not honoured, but the bona fides of the set-off or counterclaim were questionable, or the amount of those counterclaims was, in any event, inferior to the amount awarded by the adjudicator.

In *SL Sethia Liners Ltd v Naviagro Maritima Corporation Ltd (The Kostas Melas)*,[2] the courts upheld an interim award of an arbitrator of approximately

---

1    Part of art 5 – settlement of disputes arbitration from JCT 80.
2    [1981] 1 Lloyd's Rep 18.

US$100,000. The arbitrator had found that the claimant was entitled to that sum as a minimum where the respondents had failed to establish the bona fides of their alleged deductions and set-offs. An interim award can, of course, be enforced as a judgment under s 66 of the Arbitration Act 1996.

## 5.9 PEREMPTORY ORDERS UNDER SECTION 41 OF THE ARBITRATION ACT 1996

Peremptory orders under s 41 of the Arbitration Act 1996 are provided for by the Scheme for Construction Contracts, which is discussed in Chapter 3.

## 5.10 CHALLENGES TO THE DECISION

As we saw in Chapter 3, the adjudicator has a duty to act impartially, which may be extended depending on the duties imposed on the adjudicator in the adjudication scheme itself. In the TeCSA Adjudication Rules 1999 Version 1.3 the adjudicator is required to act fairly and impartially; it is debatable whether this adds much to his duty to be impartial, given that he has to exercise that impartiality subject to a stringent timetable. The scope for arguing partiality against an adjudicator is restricted by the nature of his role, which is described in Chapter 4. Discussing matters directly with one of the parties in the absence of the other party, as some of the schemes provide, would not be evidence of partiality. In *Midland Montague Leasing (UK) Ltd v Tyne & Wear Passenger Transport Executive and Ernst & Whinney*,[1] an expert had to issue a certificate in a finance leasing contract. While attending a meeting with the lessors, he was present as they discussed with their solicitors tactics for dealing with the lessees. Although the court said that the expert should have remained apart from such discussions, this did not invalidate the certificate he had issued. *Macob Civil Engineering Limited v Morrison Construction Limited* demonstrated the difficulty in advancing an argument of breach of natural justice. Allegations of such a nature do not make the decision unenforceable in the meanwhile. Some commentators have suggested that the European Convention on Human Rights (incorporated into English law by the Human Rights Act 1998), in particular Article 6, the right to a fair trial, may impinge on the operation of adjudication. The salient words are:

> 'In the determination of his civil rights and obligations . . . everyone is entitled to a fair and public hearing within a reasonable time by an independent and impartial tribunal established by law.'

In our view, this is overstating the place of adjudication, which is a procedure of which the parties to a construction contract can choose to avail themselves. Although its inclusion in a construction contract is mandatory, its use is not. The adjudicator's decision is not final unless the parties want it to be. Adjudications

---

1    (Unreported) 23 February 1990, ChD.

are held in private, but then so are arbitrations, no-one has suggested (so far) that arbitration conflicts with Article 6 of the Convention.

There is one element of Article 6 that should, perhaps, prompt amendment to the Scheme and possibly the 1996 Act and that is the word 'independent'. Making it a requirement that the adjudicator should be both impartial and independent would reduce the potential for argument on this point and would negate attempts by parties with disproportionate bargaining power imposing adjudicators in contracts who were clearly not independent.

## 5.10.1 Issues of jurisdiction

A party to a construction contract has the right to refer 'a dispute' to adjudication. Leaving aside the issue of disputes over certificates deemed to be final (which are excluded under the Scheme), the dispute is described or defined in the notice of adjudication. In the Scheme, for example, this notice must include the nature, and a brief description of, a dispute, together with the nature of the redress sought. If it is clear from the adjudicator's decision that he has ruled on some other dispute between the parties which is not detailed in the notice, and which falls outside the scope of what the Scheme or the relevant sets of rules permit him to consider, he will have acted outside his jurisdiction. See **3.8.11** for commentary on the Scheme in this respect. This should not be confused with evidence which neither party has produced to the auditor, and which he may not himself have drawn to their attention. The 1996 Act makes clear, as is embodied and expanded upon in the various schemes, that the adjudicator makes his own investigations, gathers his own evidence and uses his own knowledge and/or expertise.

In *RMC Panel Products Ltd v Amec Building Ltd*,[1] the main contractor failed to comply with the adjudicator's decision given under the DOM/1 form of sub-contract. The judge considered that the reasons given by the adjudicator were doubtful, and ruled that in giving reasons he had exceeded the powers conveyed upon him under the contract.

In *Project Consultancy Group v The Trustees of the Gray Trust*,[2] Dyson J dismissed an application for summary judgment based on an adjudicator's award. There were doubts as to the jurisdiction of the arbitrator, first on the basis as to whether there was a contract at all, and, secondly, if there was a contract, whether it had been entered into before or after 1 May 1998. In the face of these doubts, Dyson J concluded that there was a real prospect of the defendants showing that the adjudicator was wrong in holding that the contract was concluded after 1 May 1998, consequently he declined to give summary judgment.

The defendants, the Trustees of the Gray Trust, made their position clear on the jurisdiction of the adjudicator from the outset. They had participated in the adjudication maintaining this reservation. They had not, as the plaintiff

---

1    (1993) unreported.
2    TCC judgment Friday, 16 July 1999, as yet unreported; available on Lawtel.

suggested, agreed to confer on the adjudicator the power to determine the issue of jurisdiction.

Dyson J did comment that he felt that there would be comparatively few cases where the advancement of the jurisdiction argument would be possible and that the court 'will be vigilant to examine the arguments critically'.

## 5.10.2 Mistake

Where the adjudicator does not give reasons for his decision, exposing a mistake will be difficult. In order to be discernible, the mistake must be serious, and consequently, may be challenged. In *Jones v Sherwood Computer Services plc*,[1] the Court of Appeal suggested that in a case concerning expert determination an example of a mistake which would warrant challenge would be valuing the shares of the wrong company. In a construction contract context, if the adjudicator reviewed and decided on a certified amount other than the one which was in dispute, that ought to be a sufficient mistake to found a challenge.

---

1     [1992] 1 WLR 277.

# Chapter 6

## INTERNATIONAL ADJUDICATION DISPUTE BOARDS

### 6.1 INTRODUCTION

In Chapter 1, mention was made of adjudication in international construction projects. In this chapter, this topic is expanded, and the concept and use of dispute boards is explained.

International construction projects vary widely in their scope and scale. Whilst they are not all huge, many of the largest construction projects in the world are properly classified as international, involving contractors and consultants from countries other than the host country. Furthermore, international construction is likely to expand in the future as Third World nations develop their infrastructure on the back of private finance.

The changing nature of project finance makes it more important than ever to control project costs and for the contracting parties and their backers to know the state of the balance sheet. If a project will take a decade to construct, which is not unusual, for example, in the case of a large dam in a remote area, both the contractor and the owner need to be certain of their financial situation throughout the construction period. Differences are almost inevitable in relation to such large projects and it is not satisfactory that those differences (if not resolved by the parties) are dependent upon an arbitrator's decision given perhaps several years after project completion. The task of reconstructing events, which occurred many years before, possibly without the assistance of those who were present at the time, is laborious, expensive and prone to inaccuracy. As such, it is far better that differences are settled as they arise while the issues are fresh in the parties' minds and before they become entangled with other matters.

It is with this in mind that dispute boards have developed. As will be explained later in this chapter, dispute boards can provide prompt, impartial, informal and cost-effective means of dispute-resolution, which is ideal for international construction projects. However, much of what follows is equally applicable to adjudication by dispute boards within the UK, although the impact of the Housing Grants, Construction and Regeneration Act 1996 (the 1996 Act) must not be overlooked.

## 6.2 HISTORY

Adjudication in international commerce is not new. Expert determination in commodity contract disputes is well established. In large construction projects, the earliest use of a dispute board is thought to have been on a dam project in the USA in the 1960s, under which an independent technical board was established to advise on design and constructional aspects of the job. At completion, several disputes were unresolved and the parties, by this time confident in the ability of the technical board, requested advice on how the disputes could be resolved. In consequence, a dispute review board (DRB) was created.

The success of this first DRB led to its use on other projects in the USA, particularly those involving underground construction where the likelihood of disputes was great. Government agencies were encouraged to use dispute boards, and it was inevitable that this trend would develop outside the USA. In the early 1980s, a project to construct a high concrete arch dam was commenced in Honduras. The Hondurans, who had engaged American advisers, awarded contracts to European contractors. A number of disputes arose and the Hondurans were persuaded to establish a DRB to hear and make recommendations on existing and future disputes. This first international DRB worked well and the recommendations made were accepted by both parties, thus avoiding arbitration.

This early success eventually led to dispute boards being used on other international construction projects, including the Channel Tunnel in the late 1980s.

The World Bank, as a major funder of international construction, realised the benefits which can arise from early dispute-resolution, and in 1995 published its recommendations for the procurement of works which included provisions for the use of dispute boards for projects of significant value. This lead was followed by the Fédération Internationale des Ingénieurs-Conseils (FIDIC) which, in 1995 and 1996, published standard form contracts and contract amendments which included provisions for the setting-up and operation of dispute adjudication boards.

The last few years have seen an upsurge in the development and use of dispute boards. In the UK, they are in use on several major railway projects including the Channel Tunnel Rail Link, numerous large road and bridge schemes and several power plants. More spectacular is their popularity on international construction projects, with dispute boards in operation in about 20 countries. In 1996, a Dispute Review Board Foundation was formed. Based in Seattle, the Foundation now has upwards of 500 individual and corporate members and branches in 14 countries, including the UK.

## 6.3 TYPICAL DISPUTE BOARD CONTRACT CLAUSES

Under the provisions of the 1996 Act, if a contract is not exempt from the Scheme[1] any adjudicator must be a named individual. However, where contracts do not fall within the Scheme, the 'adjudicator' can be a board. The 1996 Act does not apply to international projects, and the board is entirely a creature of contract, requiring the parties to agree on its formation, terms of reference and procedure for operation. There are numerous ad hoc instruments which establish dispute boards. Perhaps the best example of a standard contract incorporating adjudication by a dispute board is the FIDIC Supplement to the Fourth Edition (1987) of Conditions of Contract for Works of Civil Engineering Construction, published in 1996. This contains suggested amendments to the original FIDIC Fourth Edition clauses covering the settlement of disputes and arbitration. Clause 67 (as amended) is reproduced below in full with a commentary after each sub-clause.[2]

### 6.3.1 Settlement of disputes and arbitration

'67.1 If a dispute of any kind whatsoever arises between the Employer and the Contractor in connection with, or arising out of, the Contract or the execution of the Works, including any dispute as to any opinion, instruction, determination, certificate or valuation of the Engineer, the dispute shall initially be referred in writing to the Dispute Adjudication Board (the "Board") for its decision. Such reference shall state that it is made under this Sub-Clause.

Unless the member or members of the Board have been previously mutually agreed upon by the parties and named in the Contract, the parties shall, within 28 days of the Commencement Date, jointly ensure the appointment of the Board. The Board shall comprise suitably qualified persons as members, the number of members being either one or three, as stated in the Appendix to Tender. If the Board is to comprise three members, each party shall nominate one member for the approval of the other party, and the parties shall mutually agree upon and appoint the third member (who shall act as chairman).

The terms of appointment of the Board shall:

(a) incorporate the model terms therefor published by the Fédération Internationale des Ingénieurs-Conseils (FIDIC), as they may have been amended by the parties,
(b) require each member of the Board to be, and to remain throughout his appointment, independent of the parties,
(c) require the Board to act impartially and in accordance with the Contract, and
(d) include undertakings by the parties (to each other and to the Board) that the members of the Board shall in no circumstances be liable for anything done or omitted in the discharge of their functions unless the act or omission is shown to have been in bad faith; the parties shall indemnify the members against such claims.

The terms of the remuneration of each member of the Board, including the remuneration of any expert from whom the Board may seek advice, shall be mutually agreed upon by the Employer, the Contractor and each member of the Board when agreeing the terms of

---

1    Scheme for Construction Contracts (England and Wales) Regulations 1998, SI 1998/649.
2    It should be noted that 'test editions' of revised FIDIC contracts were published for discussion purposes in late 1998. Publication of these documents in their final form is anticipated in mid-1999.

appointment. In the event of disagreement, the remuneration of each member shall include a daily fee in accordance with the daily fee established from time to time for arbitrators under the administrative and financial regulations of the International Centre for Settlement of Investment Disputes, a retainer fee per calendar month equivalent to three times such daily fee and reimbursement for reasonable expenses. The Employer and the Contractor shall each be responsible for paying one-half of the Board's remuneration.

The appointment of any member of the Board may be terminated (other than on a member's own initiative) only by mutual agreement of the Employer and the Contractor. The appointment of each member of the Board shall expire when the discharge referred to in Sub-Clause 60.7 shall have become effective, or at such other time as the parties may mutually agree.

If at any time the parties agree, they may appoint a suitably qualified person or persons to replace (or to be available to replace) any or all members of the Board. Unless the parties agree otherwise, the appointment will come into effect if a member of the Board declines to act or is unable to act as a result of death, disability, resignation or termination of appointment. If any of such circumstances should occur and no such replacement is available, the member shall be replaced in the same manner as such member was nominated or agreed upon.

If any of the following conditions apply, namely:

(a)	the parties fail to agree upon the appointment of the sole member of a one-person Board within 28 days of the Commencement Date,
(b)	either party fails to nominate a member (acceptable to the other party), for a Board of three members, within 28 days of the Commencement Date,
(c)	the parties fail to agree upon the appointment of the third member (to act as chairman) for a Board of three members within 28 days of the Commencement Date, or
(d)	the parties fail to agree upon the appointment of the third member of the Board within 28 days of the date on which a member of the Board declines to act or is unable to act as a result of death, disability, resignation or termination of appointment,

then the appointing body or official named in the Appendix to Tender shall, after due consultation with the parties, appoint such member of the Board, and such appointment shall be final and conclusive.'

## Time period for setting up board

Under this sub-clause the parties agree to establish, within 28 days after the contractual commencement date, a dispute adjudication board, which is given jurisdiction, by party agreement, to decide any dispute which may arise between the parties. FIDIC suggests that projects with estimated contract prices exceeding US$25 million are suitable for a three-man board. One-man 'boards' are recommended as more appropriate for smaller projects.

## Qualification of members

Members must be suitably qualified. Adjudication is quasi-judicial in nature but a member does not need to be legally qualified to act quasi-judicially. The Institution of Civil Engineers (ICE) suite of contracts has, for over half a century, required engineers to act quasi-judicially. Many disputes referred to the board will be of a technical nature and, while these may be readily assimilated by persons experienced in construction, they may be less clear to those without such experience. However, it is recognised that lawyers who have specialised in construction law will, during their careers, acquire considerable knowledge of construction procedures, working methods, standard form construction contracts, etc. It would not, we submit, be appropriate for a non-construction lawyer to be appointed to a dispute board simply because of an understanding of judicial processes. The most successful dispute boards are those where the members can offer a range of experience relating to the project – possibly with one member having an arbitral or legal qualification.

## Procedure for choosing members

The procedure for choosing board members is relatively straightforward. It is preferable for the members to be mutually agreed before the award of the contract and it may be possible for shortlisted tenderers and the employer to exchange lists of acceptable persons (who have agreed to have their names put forward). Such an arrangement means that board members can be selected and the board established from day one. If this is not possible, selection and appointment of board members immediately after award is essential. The tendency to wait for the first dispute to arise before appointing the board should be resisted. As explained below, one major advantage in establishing a dispute board is that the board, through regular visits to the construction site, becomes familiar with the project throughout all its stages and is therefore 'up to speed' if and when disputes arise. In cases where the parties are required, post award, to select the member for a one-man board or the chairman of a three-man board, the contract should provide that, in the event of failure to agree, the selection is vested in a suitable professional organisation, such as the ICE, or, in the case of the chairman, that the selection is vested in the other two members.

An obvious pitfall is for an employer to select all the members of the board in advance of the award of contract, so that tenderers have to deal with a board which is not acceptable or is unrepresentative of all sides of the construction industry. If the employer does select board members in advance, great care should be taken in ensuring a balanced membership of genuinely independent persons. On some multi-contract projects in which dispute boards have been used, it is usual that the employer selects members in advance. In such cases, it makes good sense for the employer to seek advice and input from a professional organisation, such as the ICE, as a means of maintaining impartial selection.

In three-man boards, each party is entitled to propose one board member. Party selection should not be construed as party representation. The terms of members' appointments require the members to be, and to remain, independent of the parties and to act impartially. Dispute boards are successful only if both parties are confident of the impartiality of the board and thus believe that they will be treated fairly. Any perception that the board or a member is biased in favour of a particular party will destroy confidence and undermine the benefits a board can bring. This aspect is of vital importance and any prospective board member should declare any and all interests and affinities before accepting an appointment. In some selection processes, prospective members are required to complete a questionnaire or to make declarations of independence, previous associations with the parties and impartiality.

### Remuneration

The International Centre for Settlement of Investment Disputes (ICSID) daily rates, which are used in default of agreement of members' remuneration, are not high, the current rate being unchanged for eight years. In agreeing suitable levels of remuneration, parties should be cognisant of a member's usual daily rate (for other similar work) and the value of his experience and skill to the project.

### Termination of membership

Termination of membership of a board should be only 'for cause' and then by mutual agreement of the parties. For a member's appointment to be terminable by one (disgruntled) party and without cause is akin to a losing litigant sacking the presiding judge. Once appointed, a member remains in office throughout the contract, the board being stood down only by agreement of the parties or when payment under the final payment certificate is made.

## 6.3.2   Procedure for obtaining the board's decision

'67.2 When in accordance with Sub-Clause 67.1 a dispute is referred by one party to the Board, a copy of such reference shall be sent by that party to the other party and (for information) to the Engineer. The parties shall promptly make available to the Board all such additional information, further access to the Site, and appropriate facilities, as the Board may require for the purposes of rendering a decision.

The Board shall have full power, among other things, to:

(a)   establish the procedure to be applied in deciding a dispute,
(b)   decide upon the Board's own jurisdiction, and as to the scope of any dispute referred to it,
(c)   take the initiative in ascertaining the facts and matters required for a decision,
(d)   make use of its own specialist knowledge, if any,
(e)   decide upon the payment of interest in accordance with the Contract,
(f)   decide to grant provisional relief such as interim or conservatory measures, and
(g)   open up, review and revise any opinion, instruction, determination, certificate or valuation of the Engineer related to the dispute.

No later than the eighty-fourth day after the day on which it received such reference, the Board, acting as a panel of expert(s) and not as arbitrator(s), shall give notice of its decision, to the parties and (for information) to the Engineer. Such decision, which shall be reasoned, shall state that it is given under this Sub-Clause.

Unless the Contract has already been repudiated or terminated, the Contractor shall, in every case, continue to proceed with the Works with all due diligence, and the Contractor and the Employer, as well as the Engineer, shall give effect forthwith to every decision of the Board, unless and until the same shall be revised, as hereinafter provided, in an amicable settlement or an arbitral award.

If either party is dissatisfied with the Board's decision, then either party, on or before the twenty-eighth day after the day on which it received notice of such decision, may notify the other party and (for information) the Engineer of its dissatisfaction. If the Board fails to give notice of its decision on or before the eighty-fourth day after the day on which it received the reference, then either party, on or before the twenty-eighth day after the day on which the said period of 84 days has expired, may notify the other party and (for information) the Engineer of its dissatisfaction. In either event, such notice of dissatisfaction shall state that it is given under this Sub-Clause, and set out the matter in dispute and the reason(s) for dissatisfaction. Subject to Sub-Clauses 67.5 and 67.6, no arbitration in respect of such dispute may be commenced unless such notice is given.

If the Board has given notice of its decision as to a matter in dispute to the Employer, the Contractor and the Engineer, and no notice of dissatisfaction has been given by either party on or before the twenty-eighth day after the day on which the parties received the Board's decision, then the Board's decision shall become final and binding upon the Employer and the Contractor.'

This sub-clause describes the procedures to be followed by the party upon referral to the board of a dispute. There is no limit on the type of dispute on which a board decision can be requested; the only potential difficulty is whether a dispute has actually arisen. As such, the referring party would be well advised to notify the other party that it considers that a dispute has arisen because of 'the passage of time' since the matter arose, and the 'lack of agreement' reached to date. If such notification is reasonable in all the circumstances, it is unlikely that the board would refuse to entertain the dispute.

It is good practice for the parties to be informed by the board of exactly what their additional submissions should comprise. The timetable allowed for adjudication by the board is tight and it will frustrate the procedures and lessen the quality of the final decision if vital information is not forthcoming from the parties until late in the adjudication process. Accordingly, the board should take the time to review the original submissions upon receipt in order to seek additional information as necessary.

Under the FIDIC regime, the board is not empowered to appoint experts directly and at its own initiative. However, it is possible that the board will require expert advice on certain highly specialised matters, and the sub-clause provides that such 'facilities' are to be provided by the parties. In other words, the parties should jointly engage an outside expert when reasonably requested by the board. There is no harm in the board making suggestions as to suitable experts.

The sub-clause continues by setting out the board's powers. The FIDIC grants the board 'full' power in respect of the procedure to be adopted. However, a board should take notice of the wishes of the parties if these are agreed. Only where the board considers that procedures agreed between the parties are unworkable or would lead to unsatisfactory results should it reject the parties' proposals and adopt its own.

The board is given inquisitorial powers. It is thus required to be proactive in discovering the truth, not merely to hear and determine.

The board is declared to be a panel of experts and not arbitrators. This prevents the board being subject to the benefits and burdens of any laws governing the conduct of arbitrations (eg appeals, formalities etc) and means that its decision is not enforceable as an arbitral award. Arbitration subsequent to the board's decision is not precluded.

The final parts of the sub-clause relate to time periods and actions which may be taken after the notice of the board's decision (or lack thereof). If either party gives notice of its dissatisfaction with the board's decision within the specified time, arbitration may follow. If no such notice is given, the board's decision is final and binding on the parties.

### 6.3.3  Failure to comply with the board's decision

'67.5 Where neither party has given notice of dissatisfaction within the period in Sub-Clause 67.2 and the Board's related decision, if any, has become final and binding, either party may, if the other party fails to comply with such decision, and without prejudice to any other rights it may have, refer the failure itself to arbitration under Sub-Clause 67.4. The provisions of Sub-Clauses 67.2 and 67.3 shall not apply to any such reference.'

This sub-clause provides the coercive means by which a party can enforce a final and binding decision of the board. The sub-clause specifies arbitration as the route of enforcement, but there are no reasons why an application to the courts could not be made, although the defaulting party may seek to stay court proceedings and have the enforcement action heard by an arbitrator. Whether it is brought before an arbitrator or the courts, the decision of the board remains final and the issue is solely one of enforcement. Unless the arbitrator or the court is convinced that the board acted improperly in conducting the reference, or was in some other way unlawful in its actions, the board's decision will be adopted by the arbitrator or the court, and an award or a judgment made accordingly.

The FIDIC Supplement, in addition to containing the revised cl 67 provisions, also contains model terms of appointment and procedural rules for the dispute adjudication board. These ancillary documents are reproduced in Appendix 3 to this book.

The FIDIC dispute adjudication board provisions are still in their infancy. Several boards have been established under the FIDIC regime and, by all accounts, are working satisfactorily. In the fullness of time the FIDIC provisions will be better tested and improvements will, no doubt, be made. It should be emphasised that the FIDIC does not have a monopoly over dispute board provisions. In particular, the FIDIC model discussed above has been devised for use with the traditional procurement approach. With the recent increase in private sector infrastructure development, dispute boards are now used as a principal means of dispute-resolution between promoters and concessionaires, sometimes also being concerned with 'lower tier' disputes between concessionaire and works contractors. The dispute board provisions in these contracts are, understandably, more complex and usually project-specific.

The remaining part of this chapter considers a number of aspects concerning the establishment, operation, burdens and benefits of adjudication by dispute boards.

## 6.4   THE IMPORTANCE OF EARLY APPOINTMENT AND REGULAR SITE VISITS BY THE BOARD

The feature that distinguishes dispute boards from other forms of dispute-resolution is the continued proximity of the board to the project and the parties. By being an integral part of the project, the board is not viewed with fear or suspicion. Ideally, it should be seen as a facility to be used by the parties if and when necessary. Early establishment enables the board to influence the attitudes and behaviour of those persons involved in construction and to encourage the notion of partnering. Parties are more reluctant to take aggressive and uncompromising positions in the certain knowledge that the board will view such behaviour unfavourably. Unlike most arbitration and litigation, adjudication occurs during the construction period and may require those directly involved with the construction process to testify before the board.

Regular site visits by the board (FIDIC recommends at least three visits each year, irrespective of there being disputes) enable board members to remain conversant with all aspects of the project and to observe problems as they develop. Technical and logistical difficulties and their contractual ramifications are readily appreciated. Thereafter, if the board is required to make a decision, its close knowledge of the project will permit quick, well-informed and even-handed responses. No amount of *ex post facto* evidence can match first-hand knowledge.

Perhaps most important is the opportunity for the parties, at regular intervals, to discuss contractual issues in the presence of the board. Regular visits by the board provide a forum for either party to 'get it off his chest', and alert the other party and the board of fears and grievances at an early opportunity. Board visits are occasions where the principals of the parties are likely to be in attendance and, often for the first time, hear information on the contractual difficulties being experienced by the other party, particularly at site level. This regular review of claims and potential claims was recently referred to by Lord Woolf MR as 'lancing the boil'.[1]

While the function of the board is recognised as quasi-judicial, a visit may also present opportunities for the board to operate in a conciliatory manner and thereby avert differences which may otherwise turn into disputes. Admittedly, care must be taken and the board should not be lured into giving informal pronouncements

---

1    Keynote Speech: 'Adjudication – A New Deal for Construction Contracts' the Insitution of Civil Engineers 1997.

which effectively prejudge issues before formal notice of dispute is given. Notwithstanding that caveat, the 'informal' approach taken by a board during a visit can prove very useful in clarifying misunderstandings and misinterpretations, and permitting settlement.

The length of site visit will vary considerably. For a large project in a remote location, a visit over three or four days is not unusual. The board will view the project, receive progress updates and programme difficulties, review progress made on claims and disputes to date and, if required, convene hearings on notified disputes. Clearly, there is merit in the board combining its regular visits with hearings of disputes and, depending on the complexity and number of hearings, the visit may stretch over a longer period.

## 6.5   HEARINGS

Hearings are not always necessary, and, if submissions in writing are made by the parties, the board may prepare its decision on documents only, requesting further information as necessary. However, experience indicates that most parties to a dispute prefer an occasion at which an oral presentation can be given, supported by written skeleton arguments. Consequently, hearings are normal and are clearly necessary if the board wishes to put questions to the parties or to others involved in the construction process.

Hearings should be relatively informal, and more akin to a site meeting than a court of law. Position papers will usually have been supplied by both parties and the hearing commences with each party being given an opportunity to present an opening statement in support of its main contentions. Inevitably, the other party will wish to respond, and the board will ask questions. The number of rounds of exchanges is variable although the board should be vigilant in ensuring that there is no repetition. It is important that both sides leave the hearing confident that their cases has been fully explained to the board.

Some dispute board provisions deny the parties any right of cross-examination – all questioning being at the initiative of the board itself. In other cases, cross-questioning is permitted, although the board should ensure this is carried out in an orderly manner, particularly when the parties' presenters are likely to be construction personnel and not trained advocates.

## 6.6   PROCEDURES AND THE CHAIRMAN'S ROLE

Dispute board procedures should be simple and efficient. To impose multiple steps of review and negotiation prior to or during the adjudication process can increase confrontation and lessen the chances of success. However, the board must be firm as well as being fair, much of the responsibility for this resting upon the chairman.

Under the FIDIC regime a standard set of procedures is adopted. In other cases, it is essential that the board ensures that a written set of procedures is prepared and, if possible, agreed by the parties. Whenever possible, the wishes of the parties should be incorporated, although the final decision must be that of the board.

The chairman plays a pivotal role in the successful operation and functioning of the board. He must chair all meetings and know precisely the issues that should receive most attention during the limited time the members are together. He must understand both the technical and contractual issues and be prepared to lead discussions between the parties during the regular meetings and at hearings. As chairman he must, throughout the project, keep closely in touch with the other members and with the parties, striving for consensus wherever possible. Importantly, the chairman must ensure that the agreed procedure for a hearing is followed as fairly as possible and that both parties are given adequate opportunity to present their cases and answer any questions arising therefrom.

A dispute board must produce a written (and usually reasoned) decision document. While there are occasions when this document can be produced during a visit to site (where the hearing usually takes place), generally the board would consider its findings and draft its decision document in the weeks following the hearing. The chairman is responsible for convening any post-hearing meetings of the board and in ensuring that the final decision document is produced within the time-limits laid down and that it comprehensively covers the matters in contention.

## 6.7   WHY DO DISPUTE BOARDS WORK?

Based on experience to date, dispute boards are effective in resolving construction disputes for a number of reasons. The parties are required to operate under the shadow of the board and efforts are thus made to resolve potential disputes and reduce matters in contention without recourse to the board; neither party wishing to lose at a hearing.

Personnel involved in the construction are aware that their behaviour during the contract will be monitored by the board and inferences will be drawn; the temptation to write an acrimonious letter or take up an entrenched attitude may be resisted in the knowledge that the board is watching. Hence, relationships do not become as strained as might otherwise be the case.

Related to this is the desire that the parties remain credible in the eyes of the board. Consequently, the parties will undertake a 'reality check' on issues to be put to the board. Spurious claims – or defences – will not pass the check and will not be advanced.

Where an owner includes provisions for the existence of a dispute board in the bidding documents, tenderers are given an indication that fair play will prevail, which can promote a spirit of openness and partnering.

Construction personnel have strong paternalistic feelings towards their projects. During regular visits of the board to the site, the parties report on progress. Where this is required to be in the form of a joint report, the parties are thereby encouraged to work together and take efforts to make their project appear successful to the board. Again, the spirit of partnering is encouraged.

When a dispute does arise, the ability to refer the matter to a standing board enables disputes to be handled piecemeal. If a dispute board is used effectively, matters of principle should be referred as they arise and disputes should not be allowed to develop into huge compendium claims. In this way, issues remain isolated and self-contained. Adjudication is best undertaken in bite-sized pieces. Decisions given in one dispute may have applicability in several others and may assist in amicable settlements being reached.

The board's familiarity with the project and the contractual issues means that the background to any dispute is well known to the members. The board should have no need for historical facts to be reconstructed (as would be necessary for an arbitrator or judge), thus saving time and cost. Furthermore, the time taken in case preparation and at the hearing is greatly reduced compared to what is typical in arbitration. As disputes can be addressed contemporaneously, site personnel are usually available for questioning. Overall, more certainty exists and the final decision of the board is considered as good if not better than that of an arbitrator or judge. Consequently, parties are more likely to accept the decision without rancour.

Over the course of a project the board may be called upon numerous times to adjudicate disputes. It is likely that decisions will go both ways. The favourable decisions tend to dissuade a party from challenging those which are unfavourable.

The confidential, low-key procedures of the dispute board process help preserve good site relationships. The board can provide face-saving options whenever possible and avoid embarrassment or further confrontation between the parties.

Finally, the costs of establishing a dispute board are considered reasonable when compared to the benefit they bring. The costs of a dispute board for a lengthy and complex project are likely to be far less than the unrecoverable costs of even a single arbitration. Dispute boards are, therefore, good value for money.

## 6.8 CONCLUSION

Adjudication has taken its place firmly in the international construction arena. It is likely that most major international projects will consider setting up a dispute board. Whether or not procurement is by traditional means, the dispute board concept can be tailored to benefit a project. Several long-term concession projects, still in the course of planning, aim to establish dispute boards for the length of the concession; in some cases upwards of 25 years. Clearly, this could only be effected with a 'moving' membership.

Adjudication, does not, however, guarantee that a dispute will be resolved. The speed and informality of the adjudication process mean that adjudication cannot be as detailed or thorough as arbitration or litigation. It is recognised as a quick-fix solution and there will be occasions, hopefully few, where the aggrieved party will decide to proceed to arbitration, particularly if the time-limits set for the adjudication have been insufficient for the adjudicator to absorb all of the information presented.

At the start of this chapter, it was forecast that international construction will continue to grow. With this growth, it is inevitable that there will be a development and more widespread use of dispute boards.

# Chapter 7

## FUTURE DEVELOPMENTS

### 7.1 CHANGES TO THE 1996 ACT TO PROVIDE FOR THE SCOPE OF CONSTRUCTION CONTRACTS

The first 12 months since the implementation of the 1996 Act have not witnessed the anticipated flood of adjudications that some commentators expected, nor have they thrown up to public gaze the sort of problems which we have touched on earlier in this book. This may be attributable to natural caution in using a procedure which is new, untried and untested; or, people may prefer to learn from the experience and mistakes of others before embarking upon adjudication themselves; or the relatively small number of adjudications may be attributable to the success of adjudication: parties who are in dispute, particularly the potential paying party, know that if that dispute is not resolved they can face being embroiled immediately in an adjudication with a decision in a very short space of time. Equally, a number of adjudications have, no doubt, been initiated but then have settled, as has always been the case with many arbitrations.

To date, there has been no pressure to extend the scope of adjudications to contracts which are currently excluded. Indeed, anecdotal evidence would suggest that, where adjudications have been initiated, it has been between main contractors and sub-contractors where there was already adjudication, albeit limited, under the JCT Sub-Contract Forms.

### 7.2 THE ENFORCEABILITY OF ADJUDICATION AWARDS

One of the concerns expressed during the original passage of legislation through Parliament concerned the enforceability of adjudication awards. This was a particular concern, for example, of ORSA, now the Technology and Construction Court Solicitors Association ('TeCSA') who, amongst others, pressed strongly for an adjudicators' decision to be accorded a special status, akin to the system of registration for abitration awards. In the event, no such special privileges were accorded to adjudicators' decisions. Enforcement would have to be by way of an application to the Court for an appropriate order, be that an injunction or a summary judgment.

Some standard form contracts, the JCT Standard Forms being one, excluded the enforcement of adjudicators' decisions from the scope of their arbitration clauses. This we discussed at **5.7**. Some compliance schemes, which we examined in detail at **3.2** to **3.6**, excluded the rights of set-off and counterclaim or abatement when the adjudicators' decision came to be enforced. This is particularly the case of the ORSA Scheme 2.1.

The first judgment on the enforcement of adjudicators' decision was made on 12 February 1999. *Macob Civil Engineering Limited v Morrison Construction Limited* was heard by Dyson J, the head of the TCC. This decision is examined in some length in Chapter 5. Dyson J took a purposive approach to the interpretation of the 1996 Act and, in doing so, circumvented a number of the problems that had been seen with enforcement. He upheld the right to have the adjudicators' decision immediately enforced, either by way of an injunction where appropriate, or more usually by means of an application for summary judgment.

This decision will give great heart to those who have been concerned about enforcement and may well encourage a greater use of the procedure. Significantly, it involved a contract which did not fully comply with the 1996 Act and therefore the government Scheme applied. The arbitration clause in the contract did not exclude from its scope the enforcement of adjudicators' decisions.

What remain to be tested by the courts are some of the contractual amendments, and, some would say, abuses, that have been incorporated in some construction contracts in order to reduce or even nullify the effect of adjudicators' decisions. These range, on the one hand, from making it mandatory for any money that an adjudicator's decision orders should be paid to be deposited in a stakeholder account pending the final determination of the dispute, to clauses which purport to exclude a large number of issues from the adjudicators' jurisdiction.

The Minister for Construction, Nick Raynsford, has called for a report on such contractual amendments but, short of imposing an approved standard form contract upon everyone in the industry, it remains to be seen what legislation alone can do. What would give the impetus to challenge the more obvious abuses will be a definitive and purposive ruling from the courts on one of these contracts.

# Appendix 1

## LEGISLATION

### Contents

# HOUSING GRANTS, CONSTRUCTION AND REGENERATION ACT 1996, ss 104–117

## PART II
## CONSTRUCTION CONTRACTS

*Introductory provisions*

**104   Construction contracts**

(1) In this Part a 'construction contract' means an agreement with a person for any of the following–

(a) the carrying out of construction operations;

(b) arranging for the carrying out of construction operations by others, whether under sub-contract to him or otherwise;

(c) providing his own labour, or the labour of others, for the carrying out of construction operations.

(2) References in this Part to a construction contract include an agreement–

(a) to do architectural, design, or surveying work, or

(b) to provide advice on building, engineering, interior or exterior decoration or on the laying-out of landscape,

in relation to construction operations.

(3) References in this Part to a construction contract do not include a contract of employment (within the meaning of the Employment Rights Act 1996).

(4) The Secretary of State may by order add to, amend or repeal any of the provisions of subsection (1), (2) or (3) as to the agreements which are construction contracts for the purposes of this Part or are to be taken or not to be taken as included in references to such contracts.

No such order shall be made unless a draft of it has been laid before and approved by a resolution of each House of Parliament.

(5) Where an agreement relates to construction operations and other matters, this Part applies to it only so far as it relates to construction operations.

An agreement relates to construction operations so far as it makes provision of any kind within subsection (1) or (2).

(6) This Part applies only to construction contracts which–

(a) are entered into after the commencement of this Part, and

(b) relate to the carrying out of construction operations in England, Wales or Scotland.

(7) This Part applies whether or not the law of England and Wales or Scotland is otherwise the applicable law in relation to the contract.

**105   Meaning of 'construction operations'**

(1) In this Part 'construction operations' means, subject as follows, operations of any of the following descriptions–

(a) construction, alteration, repair, maintenance, extension, demolition or dismantling of buildings, or structures forming, or to form, part of the land (whether permanent or not);

(b) construction, alteration, repair, maintenance, extension, demolition or dismantling of any works forming, or to form, part of the land, including (without prejudice to the foregoing) walls, roadworks, power-lines, telecommunication apparatus, aircraft runways, docks and harbours, railways, inland waterways, pipe-lines, reservoirs, water-mains, wells, sewers, industrial plant and installations for purposes of land drainage, coast protection or defence;

(c) installation in any building or structure of fittings forming part of the land, including (without prejudice to the foregoing) systems of heating, lighting, air-conditioning, ventilation, power supply, drainage, sanitation, water supply or fire protection, or security or communications systems;

(d) extenal or internal cleaning of buildings and structures, so far as carried out in the course of their construction, alteration, repair, extension or restoration;

(e) operations which form an integral part of, or are preparatory to, or are for rendering complete, such operations as are previously described in this subsection, including site clearance, earth-moving, excavation, tunnelling and boring, laying of foundations, erection, maintenance or dismantling of scaffolding, site restoration, landscaping and the provision of roadways and other access works;

(f) painting or decorating the internal or external surfaces of any building or structure.

(2) The following operations are not construction operations within the meaning of this Part–

(a) drilling for, or extraction of, oil or natural gas;

(b) extraction (whether by underground or surface working) of minerals; tunnelling or boring, or construction of underground works, for this purpose;

(c) assembly, installation or demolition of plant or machinery, or erection or demolition of steelwork for the purposes of supporting or providing access to plant or machinery, on a site where the primary activity is–

   (i) nuclear processing, power generation, or water or effluent treatment, or

   (ii) the production, transmission, processing or bulk storage (other than warehousing) of chemicals, pharmaceuticals, oil, gas, steel or food and drink;

(d) manufacture or delivery to site of–

   (i) building or engineering components or equipment,

   (ii) materials, plant or machinery, or

   (iii) components for systems of heating, lighting, air-conditioning, ventilation, power supply, drainage, sanitation, water supply or fire protection, or for security or communications systems,

except under a contract which also provides for their installation;

(e) the making, installation and repair of artistic works, being sculptures, murals and other works which are wholly artistic in nature.

(3) The Secretary of State may by order add to, amend or repeal any of the provisions of subsection (1) or (2) as to the operations and work to be treated as construction operations for the purposes of this Part.

(4) No such order shall be made unless a draft of it has been laid before and approved by a resolution of each House of Parliament.

## 106  Provisions not applicable to contract with residential occupier

(1) This Part does not apply–

(a) to a construction contract with a residential occupier (see below), or

(b) to any other description of construction contract excluded from the operation of this Part by order of the Secretary of State.

(2) A construction contract with a residential occupier means a construction contract which principally relates to operations on a dwelling which one of the parties to the contract occupies, or intends to occupy, as his residence.

In this subsection 'dwelling' means a dwelling-house or a flat; and for this purpose–

'dwelling-house' does not include a building containing a flat; and

'flat' means separate and self-contained premises constructed or adapted for use for residential purposes and forming part of a building from some other part of which the premises are divided horizontally.

(3) The Secretary of State may by order amend subsection (2).

(4) No order under this section shall be made unless a draft of it has been laid before and approved by a resolution of each House of Parliament.

**107   Provisions applicable only to agreements in writing**

(1) The provisions of this Part apply only where the construction contract is in writing, and any other agreement between the parties as to any matter is effective for the purposes of this Part only if in writing.

The expressions 'agreement', 'agree' and 'agreed' shall be construed accordingly.

(2) There is an agreement in writing—

(a) if the agreement is made in writing (whether or not it is signed by the parties),
(b) if the agreement is made by exchange of communications in writing, or
(c) if the agreement is evidenced in writing.

(3) Where parties agree otherwise than in writing by reference to terms which are in writing, they make an agreement in writing.

(4) An agreement is evidenced in writing if an agreement made otherwise than in writing is recorded by one of the parties, or by a third party, with the authority of the parties to the agreement.

(5) An exchange of written submissions in adjudication proceedings, or in arbitral or legal proceedings in which the existence of an agreement otherwise than in writing is alleged by one party against another party and not denied by the other party in his response constitutes as between those parties an agreement in writing to the effect alleged.

(6) References in this Part to anything being written or in writing include its being recorded by any means.

*Adjudication*

**108   Right to refer disputes to adjudication**

(1) A party to a construction contract has the right to refer a dispute arising under the contract for adjudication under a procedure complying with this section.

For this purpose 'dispute' includes any difference.

(2) The contract shall–
(a) enable a party to give notice at any time of his intention to refer a dispute to adjudication;
(b) provide a timetable with the object of securing the appointment of the adjudicator and referral of the dispute to him within 7 days of such notice;
(c) require the adjudicator to reach a decision within 28 days of referral or such longer period as is agreed by the parties after the dispute has been referred;
(d) allow the adjudicator to extend the period of 28 days by up to 14 days, with the consent of the party by whom the dispute was referred;
(e) impose a duty on the adjudicator to act impartially; and

(f) enable the adjudicator to take the initiative in ascertaining the facts and the law.

(3) The contract shall provide that the decision of the adjudicator is binding until the dispute is finally determined by legal proceedings, by arbitration (if the contract provides for arbitration or the parties otherwise agree to arbitration) or by agreement.

The parties may agree to accept the decision of the adjudicator as finally determining the dispute.

(4) The contract shall also provide that the adjudicator is not liable for anything done or omitted in the discharge or purported discharge of his functions as adjudicator unless the act or omission is in bad faith, and that any employee or agent of the adjudicator is similarly protected from liability.

(5) If the contract does not comply with the requirements of subsections (1) to (4), the adjudication provisions of the Scheme for Construction Contracts apply.

(6) For England and Wales, the Scheme may apply the provisions of the Arbitration Act 1996 with such adaptations and modifications as appear to the Minister making the scheme to be appropriate.

For Scotland, the Scheme may include provision conferring powers on courts in relation to adjudication and provision relating to the enforcement of the adjudicator's decision.

*Payment*

**109   Entitlement to stage payments**

(1) A party to a construction contract is entitled to payments by instalments, stage payments or other periodic payments for any work under the contract unless–

(a) it is specified in the contract that the duration of the work is to be less than 45 days, or
(b) it is agreed between the parties that the duration of the work is estimated to be less than 45 days.

(2) The parties are free to agree the amounts of the payments and the intervals at which, or circumstances in which, they become due.

(3) In the absence of such agreement, the relevant provisions of the Scheme for Construction Contracts apply.

(4) References in the following sections to a payment under the contract include a payment by virtue of this section.

**110   Dates for payment**

(1) Every construction contract shall–

(a) provide an adequate mechanism for determining what payments become due under the contract, and when, and
(b) provide for a final date for payment in relation to any sum which becomes due.

The parties are free to agree how long the period is to be between the date on which a sum becomes due and the final date for payment.

(2) Every construction contract shall provide for the giving of notice by a party not later than five days after the date on which a payment becomes due from him under the contract, or would have become due if—

(a) the other party had carried out his obligations under the contract, and

(b) no set-off or abatement was permitted by reference to any sum claimed to be due under one or more other contracts,

specifying the amount (if any) of the payment made or proposed to be made, and the basis on which that amount was calculated.

(3) If or to the extent that a contract does not contain such provision as is mentioned in subsection (1) or (2), the relevant provisions of the Scheme for Construction Contracts apply.

**111   Notice of intention to withhold payment**

(1) A party to a construction contract may not withhold payment after the final date for payment of a sum due under the contract unless he has given an effective notice of intention to withhold payment.

The notice mentioned in section 110(2) may suffice as a notice of intention to withhold payment if it complies with the requirements of this section.

(2) To be effective such a notice must specify–

(a) the amount proposed to be withheld and the ground for withholding payment, or
(b) if there is more than one ground, each ground and the amount attributable to it,

and must be given not later than the prescribed period before the final date for payment.

(3) The parties are free to agree what that prescribed period is to be.

In the absence of such agreement, the period shall be that provided by the Scheme for Construction Contracts.

(4) Where an effective notice of intention to withhold payment is given, but on the matter being referred to adjudication it is decided that the whole or part of the amount should be paid, the decision shall be construed as requiring payment not later than–

(a) seven days from the date of the decision, or
(b) the date which apart from the notice would have been the final date for payment,

whichever is the later.

**112   Right to suspend performance for non-payment**

(1) Where a sum due under a construction contract is not paid in full by the final date for payment and no effective notice to withhold payment has been given, the person to whom the sum is due has the right (without prejudice to any other right or remedy) to suspend performance of his obligations under the contract to the party by whom payment ought to have been made ('the party in default').

(2) The right may not be exercised without first giving to the party in default at least seven days' notice of intention to suspend performance, stating the ground or grounds on which it is intended to suspend performance.

(3) The right to suspend performance ceases when the party in default makes payment in full of the amount due.

(4) Any period during which performance is suspended in pursuance of the right conferred by this section shall be disregarded in computing for the purposes of any contractual time limit the time taken, by the party exercising the right or by a third party, to complete any work directly or indirectly affected by the exercise of the right.

Where the contractual time limit is set by reference to a date rather than a period, the date shall be adjusted accordingly.

**113   Prohibition of conditional payment provisions**

(1) A provision making payment under a construction contract conditional on the payer receiving payment from a third person is ineffective, unless that third person, or any other person payment by whom is under the contract (directly or indirectly) a condition of payment by that third person, is insolvent.

(2) For the purposes of this section a company becomes insolvent–

  (a) on the making of an administration order against it under Part II of the Insolvency Act 1986,
  (b) on the appointment of an administrative receiver or a receiver or manager of its property under Chapter I of Part III of that Act, or the appointment of a receiver under Chapter II of that Part,
  (c) on the passing of a resolution for voluntary winding-up without a declaration of solvency under section 89 of that Act, or
  (d) on the making of a winding-up order under Part IV or V of that Act.

(3) For the purposes of this section a partnership becomes insolvent–

  (a) on the making of a winding-up order against it under any provision of the Insolvency Act 1986 as applied by an order under section 420 of that Act, or–
  (b) (*applies to Scotland only*).

(4) For the purposes of this section an individual becomes insolvent–

  (a) on the making of a bankruptcy order against him under Part IX of the Insolvency Act 1986, or
  (b) (*applies to Scotland only*).

(5) A company, partnership or individual shall also be treated as insolvent on the occurrence of any event corresponding to those specified in subsection (2), (3) or (4) under the law of Northern Ireland or of a country outside the United Kingdom.

(6) Where a provision is rendered ineffective by subsection (1), the parties are free to agree other terms for payment.

In the absence of such agreement, the relevant provisions of the Scheme for Construction Contracts apply.

*Supplementary provisions*

**114   The Scheme for Construction Contracts**

(1) The Minister shall by regulations make a scheme ('the Scheme for Construction Contracts') containing provision about the matters referred to in the preceding provisions of this Part.

(2) Before making any regulations under this section the Minister shall consult such persons as he thinks fit.

(3) In this section 'the Minister' means–

  (a) for England and Wales, the Secretary of State, and
  (b) for Scotland, the Lord Advocate.

(4) Where any provisions of the Scheme for Construction Contracts apply by virtue of this Part in default of contractual provision agreed by the parties, they have effect as implied terms of the contract concerned.

(5) Regulations under this section shall not be made unless a draft of them has been approved by resolution of each House of Parliament.

**115   Service of notices, etc**

(1) The parties are free to agree on the manner of service of any notice or other document required or authorised to be served in pursuance of the construction contract or for any of the purposes of this Part.

(2) If or to the extent that there is no such agreement the following provisions apply.

(3) A notice or other document may be served on a person by any effective means.

(4) If a notice or other document is addressed, pre-paid and delivered by post–

    (a) to the addressee's last known principal residence or, if he is or has been carrying on a trade, profession or business, his last known principal business address, or

    (b) where the addressee is a body corporate, to the body's registered or principal office,

it shall be treated as effectively served.

(5) This section does not apply to the service of documents for the purposes of legal proceedings, for which provision is made by rules of court.

(6) References in this Part to a notice or other document include any form of communication in writing and references to service shall be construed accordingly.

**116   Reckoning periods of time**

(1) For the purposes of this Part periods of time shall be reckoned as follows.

(2) Where an act is required to be done within a specified period after or from a specified date, the period begins immediately after that date.

(3) Where the period would include Christmas Day, Good Friday or a day which under the Banking and Financial Dealings Act 1971 is a bank holiday in England and Wales or, as the case may be, in Scotland, that day shall be excluded.

**117   Crown application**

(1) This Part applies to a construction contract entered into by or on behalf of the Crown otherwise than by or on behalf of Her Majesty in her private capacity.

(2) This Part applies to a construction contract entered into on behalf of the Duchy of Cornwall notwithstanding any Crown interest.

(3) Where a construction contract is entered into by or on behalf of Her Majesty in right of the Duchy of Lancaster, Her Majesty shall be represented, for the purposes of any adjudication or other proceedings arising out of the contract by virtue of this Part, by the Chancellor of the Duchy or such person as he may appoint.

(4) Where a construction contract is entered into on behalf of the Duchy of Cornwall, the Duke of Cornwall or the possessor for the time being of the Duchy shall be represented, for the purposes of any adjudication or other proceedings arising out of the contract by virtue of this Part, by such person as he may appoint.

# CONSTRUCTION CONTRACTS (ENGLAND AND WALES) EXCLUSION ORDER 1998

## SI 1998/648

### 1 Citation, commencement and extent

(1) This Order may be cited as the Construction Contracts (England and Wales) Exclusion Order 1998 and shall come into force at the end of the period of 8 weeks beginning with the day on which it is made ('the commencement date').

(2) This Order shall extend to England and Wales only.

### 2 Interpretation

In this Order, 'Part II' means Part II of the Housing Grants, Construction and Regeneration Act 1996.

### 3 Agreements under statute

A construction contract is excluded from the operation of Part II if it is–

(a) an agreement under section 38 (power of highway authorities to adopt by agreement) or section 278 (agreements as to execution of works) of the Highways Act 1980;

(b) an agreement under section 106 (planning obligations), 106A (modification or discharge of planning obligations) or 299A (Crown planning obligations) of the Town and Country Planning Act 1990;

(c) an agreement under section 104 of the Water Industry Act 1991 (agreements to adopt sewer, drain or sewage disposal works); or

(d) an externally financed development agreement within the meaning of section 1 of the National Health Service (Private Finance) Act 1997 (powers of NHS Trusts to enter into agreements).

### 4 Private finance initiative

(1) A construction contract is excluded from the operation of Part II if it is a contract entered into under the private finance initiative, within the meaning given below.

(2) A contract is entered into under the private finance initiative if all the following conditions are fulfilled–

(a) it contains a statement that it is entered into under that initiative or, as the case may be, under a project applying similar principles;

(b) the consideration due under the contract is determined at least in part by reference to one or more of the following–

(i) the standards attained in the performance of a service, the provision of which is the principal purpose or one of the principal purposes for which the building or structure is constructed;

(ii) the extent, rate or intensity of use of all or any part of the building or structure in question; or

(iii) the right to operate any facility in connection with the building or structure in question; and

(c) one of the parties to the contract is–

(i) a Minister of the Crown;

    (ii) a department in respect of which appropriation accounts are required to be prepared under the Exchequer and Audit Departments Act 1866;

   (iii) any other authority or body whose accounts are required to be examined and certified by or are open to the inspection of the Comptroller and Auditor General by virtue of an agreement entered into before the commencement date or by virtue of any enactment;

   (iv) any authority or body listed in Schedule 4 to the National Audit Act 1983 (nationalised industries and other public authorities);

   (v) a body whose accounts are subject to audit by auditors appointed by the Audit Commission;

   (vi) the governing body or trustees of a voluntary school within the meaning of section 31 of the Education Act 1996 (county schools and voluntary schools), or

  (vii) a company wholly owned by any of the bodies described in paragraphs (i) to (v).

## 5   Finance agreements

(1) A construction contract is excluded from the operation of Part II if it is a finance agreement, within the meaning given below.

(2) A contract is a finance agreement if it is any one of the following–

   (a) any contract of insurance;

   (b) any contract under which the principal obligations include the formation or dissolution of a company, unincorporated association or partnership;

   (c) any contract under which the principal obligations include the creation or transfer of securities or any right or interest in securities;

   (d) any contract under which the principal obligations include the lending of money;

   (e) any contract under which the principal obligations include an undertaking by a person to be responsible as surety for the debt or default of another person, including a fidelity bond, advance payment bond, retention bond or performance bond.

## 6   Development agreements

(1) A construction contract is excluded from the operation of Part II if it is a development agreement, within the meaning given below.

(2) A contract is a development agreement if it includes provision for the grant or disposal of a relevant interest in the land on which take place the principal construction operations to which the contract relates.

(3) In paragraph (2) above, a relevant interest in land means–

   (a) a freehold; or

   (b) a leasehold for a period which is to expire no earlier than 12 months after the completion of the construction operations under the contract.

# SCHEME FOR CONSTRUCTION CONTRACTS (ENGLAND AND WALES) REGULATIONS 1998

## SI 1998/649

### 1  Citation, commencement, extent and interpretation

(1) These Regulations may be cited as the Scheme for Construction Contracts (England and Wales) Regulations 1998 and shall come into force at the end of the period of 8 weeks beginning with the day on which they are made (the 'commencement date').

(2) These Regulations shall extend only to England and Wales.

(3) In these Regulations, 'the Act' means the Housing Grants, Construction and Regeneration Act 1996.

### 2  The Scheme for Construction Contracts

Where a construction contract does not comply with the requirements of section 108(1) to (4) of the Act, the adjudication provisions in Part I of the Schedule to these Regulations shall apply.

**3** Where–

- (a) the parties to a construction contract are unable to reach agreement for the purposes mentioned respectively in sections 109, 111 and 113 of the Act, or
- (b) a construction contract does not make provision as required by section 110 of the Act,

the relevant provisions in Part II of the Schedule to these Regulations shall apply.

**4** The provisions in the Schedule to these Regulations shall be the Scheme for Construction Contracts for the purposes of section 114 of the Act.

## SCHEDULE

### THE SCHEME FOR CONSTRUCTION CONTRACTS
### PART I – ADJUDICATION

### 1  Notice of intention to seek adjudication

(1) Any party to a construction contract (the 'referring party') may give written notice (the 'notice of adjudication') of his intention to refer any dispute arising under the contract, to adjudication.

(2) The notice of adjudication shall be given to every other party to the contract.

(3) The notice of adjudication shall set out briefly–

- (a) the nature and a brief description of the dispute and of the parties involved,
- (b) details of where and when the dispute has arisen,
- (c) the nature of the redress which is sought, and
- (d) the names and addresses of the parties to the contract (including, where appropriate, the addresses which the parties have specified for the giving of notices).

**2**–(1) Following the giving of a notice of adjudication and subject to any agreement between the parties to the dispute as to who shall act as adjudicator –

- (a) the referring party shall request the person (if any) specified in the contract to act as adjudicator, or

(b) if no person is named in the contract or the person named has already indicated that he is unwilling or unable to act, and the contract provides for a specified nominating body to select a person, the referring party shall request the nominating body named in the contract to select a person to act as adjudicator, or

(c) where neither paragraph (a) nor (b) above applies, or where the person referred to in (a) has already indicated that he is unwilling or unable to act and (b) does not apply, the referring party shall request an adjudicator nominating body to select a person to act as adjudicator.

(2) A person requested to act as adjudicator in accordance with the provisions of paragraph (1) shall indicate whether or not he is willing to act within two days of receiving the request.

(3) In this paragraph, and in paragraphs 5 and 6 below, an 'adjudicator nominating body' shall mean a body (not being a natural person and not being a party to the dispute) which holds itself out publicly as a body which will select an adjudicator when requested to do so by a referring party.

**3** The request referred to in paragraphs 2, 5 and 6 shall be accompanied by a copy of the notice of adjudication.

**4** Any person requested or selected to act as adjudicator in accordance with paragraphs 2, 5 or 6 shall be a natural person acting in his personal capacity. A person requested or selected to act as an adjudicator shall not be an employee of any of the parties to the dispute and shall declare any interest, financial or otherwise, in any matter relating to the dispute.

**5**–(1) The nominating body referred to in paragraphs 2(1)(b) and 6(1)(b) or the adjudicator nominating body referred to in paragraphs 2(1)(c), 5(2)(b) and 6(1)(c) must communicate the selection of an adjudicator to the referring party within five days of receiving a request to do so.

(2) Where the nominating body or the adjudicator nominating body fails to comply with paragraph (1), the referring party may –

(a) agree with the other party to the dispute to request a specified person to act as adjudicator, or

(b) request any other adjudicator nominating body to select a person to act as adjudicator.

(3) The person requested to act as adjudicator in accordance with the provisions of paragraphs (1) or (2) shall indicate whether or not he is willing to act within two days of receiving the request.

**6**–(1) Where an adjudicator who is named in the contract indicates to the parties that he is unable or unwilling to act, or where he fails to respond in accordance with paragraph 2(2), the referring party may –

(a) request another person (if any) specified in the contract to act as adjudicator, or

(b) request the nominating body (if any) referred to in the contract to select a person to act as adjudicator, or

(c) request any other adjudicator nominating body to select a person to act as adjudicator.

(2) The person requested to act in accordance with the provisions of paragraph (1) shall indicate whether or not he is willing to act within two days of receiving the request.

**7**–(1) Where an adjudicator has been selected in accordance with paragraphs 2, 5 or 6, the referring party shall, not later than seven days from the date of the notice of adjudication, refer the dispute in writing (the 'referral notice') to the adjudicator.

(2) A referral notice shall be accompanied by copies of, or relevant extracts from, the construction contract and such other documents as the referring party intends to rely upon.

(3) The referring party shall, at the same time as he sends to the adjudicator the documents referred to in paragraphs (1) and (2), send copies of those documents to every other party to the dispute.

**8**–(1) The adjudicator may, with the consent of all the parties to those disputes, adjudicate at the same time on more than one dispute under the same contract.

(2) The adjudicator may, with the consent of all the parties to those disputes, adjudicate at the same time on related disputes under different contracts, whether or not one or more of those parties is a party to those disputes.

(3) All the parties in paragraphs (1) and (2) respectively may agree to extend the period within which the adjudicator may reach a decision in relation to all or any of these disputes.

(4) Where an adjudicator ceases to act because a dispute is to be adjudicated on by another person in terms of this paragraph, that adjudicator's fees and expenses shall be determined in accordance with paragraph 25.

**9**–(1) An adjudicator may resign at any time on giving notice in writing to the parties to the dispute.

(2) An adjudicator must resign where the dispute is the same or substantially the same as one which has previously been referred to adjudication, and a decision has been taken in that adjudication.

(3) Where an adjudicator ceases to act under paragraph 9(1) –

    (a) the referring party may serve a fresh notice under paragraph 1 and shall request an adjudicator to act in accordance with paragraphs 2 to 7; and
    (b) if requested by the new adjudicator and insofar as it is reasonably practicable, the parties shall supply him with copies of all documents which they had made available to the previous adjudicator.

(4) Where an adjudicator resigns in the circumstances referred to in paragraph (2), or where a dispute varies significantly from the dispute referred to him in the referral notice and for that reason he is not competent to decide it, the adjudicator shall be entitled to the payment of such reasonable amount as he may determine by way of fees and expenses reasonably incurred by him. The parties shall be jointly and severally liable for any sum which remains outstanding following the making of any determination on how the payment shall be apportioned.

**10** Where any party to the dispute objects to the appointment of a particular person as adjudicator, that objection shall not invalidate the adjudicator's appointment nor any decision he may reach in accordance with paragraph 20.

**11**–(1) The parties to a dispute may at any time agree to revoke the appointment of the adjudicator. The adjudicator shall be entitled to the payment of such reasonable amount as he may determine by way of fees and expenses incurred by him. The parties shall be jointly and severally liable for any sum which remains outstanding following the making of any determination on how the payment shall be apportioned.

(2) Where the revocation of the appointment of the adjudicator is due to the default or misconduct of the adjudicator, the parties shall not be liable to pay the adjudicator's fees and expenses.

## 12  Powers of the adjudicator

The adjudicator shall –

(a) act impartially in carrying out his duties and shall do so in accordance with any relevant terms of the contract and shall reach his decision in accordance with the applicable law in relation to the contract; and

(b) avoid incurring unnecessary expense.

**13** The adjudicator may take the initiative in ascertaining the facts and the law necessary to determine the dispute, and shall decide on the procedure to be followed in the adjudication. In particular he may –

(a) request any party to the contract to supply him with such documents as he may reasonably require including, if he so directs, any written statement from any party to the contract supporting or supplementing the referral notice and any other documents given under paragraph 7(2),

(b) decide the language or languages to be used in the adjudication and whether a translation of any document is to be provided and if so by whom,

(c) meet and question any of the parties to the contract and their representatives,

(d) subject to obtaining any necessary consent from a third party or parties, make such site visits and inspections as he considers appropriate, whether accompanied by the parties or not,

(e) subject to obtaining any necessary consent from a third party or parties, carry out any tests or experiments,

(f) obtain and consider such representations and submissions as he requires, and, provided he has notified the parties of his intention, appoint experts, assessors or legal advisers,

(g) give directions as to the timetable for the adjudication, any deadlines, or limits as to the length of written documents or oral representations to be complied with, and

(h) issue other directions relating to the conduct of the adjudication.

**14** The parties shall comply with any request or direction of the adjudicator in relation to the adjudication.

**15** If, without showing sufficient cause, a party fails to comply with any request, direction or timetable of the adjudicator made in accordance with his powers, fails to produce any document or written statement requested by the adjudicator, or in any other way fails to comply with a requirement under these provisions relating to the adjudication, the adjudicator may –

(a) continue the adjudication in the absence of that party or of the document or written statement requested,

(b) draw such inferences from that failure to comply as circumstances may, in the adjudicator's opinion, be justified, and

(c) make a decision on the basis of the information before him attaching such weight as he thinks fit to any evidence submitted to him outside any period he may have requested or directed.

**16**–(1) Subject to any agreement between the parties to the contrary, and to the terms of paragraph (2) below, any party to the dispute may be assisted by, or represented by, such advisers or representatives (whether legally qualified or not) as he considers appropriate.

(2) Where the adjudicator is considering oral evidence or representations, a party to the dispute may not be represented by more than one person, unless the adjudicator gives directions to the contrary.

**17** The adjudicator shall consider any relevant information submitted to him by any of the parties to the dispute and shall make available to them any information to be taken into account in reaching his decision.

**18** The adjudicator and any party to the dispute shall not disclose to any other person any information or document provided to him in connection with the adjudication which the party supplying it has indicated is to be treated as confidential, except to the extent that it is necessary for the purposes of, or in connection with, the adjudication.

**19**–(1) The adjudicator shall reach his decision not later than –

  (a) twenty eight days after the date of the referral notice mentioned in paragraph 7(1), or
  (b) forty two days after the date of the referral notice if the referring party so consents, or
  (c) such period exceeding twenty eight days after the referral notice as the parties to the dispute may, after the giving of that notice, agree.

(2) Where the adjudicator fails, for any reason, to reach his decision in accordance with paragraph (1)

  (a) any of the parties to the dispute may serve a fresh notice under paragraph 1 and shall request an adjudicator to act in accordance with paragraphs 2 to 7; and
  (b) if requested by the new adjudicator and insofar as it is reasonably practicable, the parties shall supply him with copies of all documents which they had made available to the previous adjudicator.

(3) As soon as possible after he has reached a decision, the adjudicator shall deliver a copy of that decision to each of the parties to the contract.

**20   Adjudicator's decision**

The adjudicator shall decide the matters in dispute. He may take into account any other matters which the parties to the dispute agree should be within the scope of the adjudication or which are matters under the contract which he considers are necessarily connected with the dispute. In particular, he may –

  (a) open up, revise and review any decision taken or any certificate given by any person referred to in the contract unless the contract states that the decision or certificate is final and conclusive,
  (b) decide that any of the parties to the dispute is liable to make a payment under the contract (whether in sterling or some other currency) and, subject to section 111(4) of the Act, when that payment is due and the final date for payment,
  (c) having regard to any term of the contract relating to the payment of interest decide the circumstances in which, and the rates at which, and the periods for which simple or compound rates of interest shall be paid.

**21** In the absence of any directions by the adjudicator relating to the time for performance of his decision, the parties shall be required to comply with any decision of the adjudicator immediately on delivery of the decision to the parties in accordance with this paragraph.

**22** If requested by one of the parties to the dispute, the adjudicator shall provide reasons for his decision.

**23   Effects of the decision**

(1) In his decision, the adjudicator may, if he thinks fit, order any of the parties to comply peremptorily with his decision or any part of it.

(2) The decision of the adjudicator shall be binding on the parties, and they shall comply with it until the dispute is finally determined by legal proceedings, by arbitration (if the contract provides for arbitration or the parties otherwise agree to arbitration) or by agreement between the parties.

**24** Section 42 of the Arbitration Act 1996 shall apply to this Scheme subject to the following modifications –

  (a)  in subsection (2) for the word 'tribunal' wherever it appears there shall be substituted the word 'adjudicator',

  (b)  in subparagraph (b) of subsection (2) for the words 'arbitral proceedings' there shall be substituted the word 'adjudication',

  (c)  subparagraph (c) of subsection (2) shall be deleted, and

  (d)  subsection 93) shall be deleted.

**25** The adjudicator shall be entitled to the payment of such reasonable amount as he may determine by way of fees and expenses reasonably incurred by him. The parties shall be jointly and severally liable for any sum which remains outstanding following the making of any determination on how the payment shall be apportioned.

**26** The adjudicator shall not be liable for anything done or omitted in the discharge or purported discharge of his functions as adjudicator unless the act or omission is in bad faith, and any employee or agent of the adjudicator shall be similarly protected from liability.

## PART II–PAYMENT

### 1   Entitlement to and amount of stage payments

Where the parties to a relevant construction contract fail to agree –

  (a)  the amount of any instalment or stage or periodic payment for any work under the contract, or

  (b)  the intervals at which, or circumstances in which, such payments become due under that contract, or

  (c)  both of the matters mentioned in sub-paragraphs (a) and (b) above,

the relevant provisions of paragraphs 2 to 4 below shall apply.

**2**–(1) The amount of any payment by way of instalments or stage or periodic payments in respect of a relevant period shall be the difference between the amount determined in accordance with sub-paragraph (2) and the amount determined in accordance with sub-paragraph (3).

(2) The aggregate of the following amounts –

  (a)  an amount equal to the value of any work performed in accordance with the relevant construction contract during the period from the commencement of the contract to the end of the relevant period (excluding any amount calculated in accordance with sub-paragraph (b)),

  (b)  where the contract provides for payment for materials, an amount equal to the value of any materials manufactured on site or brought onto site for the purposes of the works during the period from the commencement of the contract to the end of the relevant period, and

  (c)  any other amount or sum which the contract specifies shall be payable during or in respect of the period from the commencement of the contract to the end of the relevant period.

(3) The aggregate of any sums which have been paid or are due for payment by way of instalments, stage or periodic payments during the period from the commencement of the contract to the end of the relevant period.

(4) An amount calculated in accordance with this paragraph shall not exceed the difference between –

  (a)  the contract price, and

  (b)  the aggregate of the instalments or stage or periodic payments which have become due.

## 3  Dates for payment

Where the parties to a construction contract fail to provide an adequate mechanism for determining either what payments become due under the contract, or when they become due for payment, or both, the relevant provisions of paragraphs 4 to 7 shall apply.

**4** Any payment of a kind mentioned in paragraph 2 above shall become due on whichever of the following dates occurs later –

    (a) the expiry of 7 days following the relevant period mentioned in paragraph 2(1) above, or

    (b) the making of a claim by the payee.

**5** The final payment payable under a relevant construction contract, namely the payment of an amount equal to the difference (if any) between –

    (a) the contract price, and

    (b) the aggregate of any instalment or stage or periodic payments which have become due under the contract,

shall become due on the expiry of –

    (a) 30 days following completion of the work, or

    (b) the making of a claim by the payee,

whichever is the later.

**6** Payment of the contract price under a construction contract (not being a relevant construction contract) shall become due on

    (a) the expiry of 30 days following the completion of the work, or

    (b) the making of a claim by the payee,

whichever is the later.

**7** Any other payment under a construction contract shall become due

    (a) on the expiry of 7 days following the completion of the work to which the payment relates, or

    (b) the making of a claim by the payee,

whichever is the later.

## 8  Final date for payment

(1) Where the parties to a construction contract fail to provide a final date for payment in relation to any sum which becomes due under a construction contract, the provisions of this paragraph shall apply.

(2) The final date for the making of any payment of a kind mentioned in paragraphs 2, 5, 6 or 7, shall be 17 days from the date that payment becomes due.

## 9  Notice specifying amount of payment

A party to a construction contract shall, not later than 5 days after the date on which any payment –

    (a) becomes due from him, or

    (b) would have become due, if –

        (i) the other party had carried out his obligations under the contract, and

        (ii) no set-off or abatement was permitted by reference to any sum claimed to be due under one or more contracts, give notice to the other party to the contract specifying the amount (if any) of the payment he has made or proposes to make, specifying to what the payment relates and the basis on which that amount is calculated.

## 10 Notice of intention to withhold payment

Any notice of intention to withhold payment mentioned in section 111 of the Act shall be given not later than the prescribed period, which is to say not later than 7 days before the final date for payment determined either in accordance with the construction contract, or where no such provision is made in the contract, in accordance with paragraph 8 above.

## 11 Prohibition of conditional payment provisions

Where a provision making payment under a construction contract conditional on the payer receiving payment from a third person is ineffective as mentioned in section 113 of the Act, and the parties have not agreed other terms for payment, the relevant provisions of –

(a) paragraphs 2, 4, 5, 7, 8, 9 and 10 shall apply in the case of a relevant construction contract, and
(b) paragraphs 6, 7, 8, 9 and 10 shall apply in the case of any other construction contract.

## 12 Interpretation

In this Part of the Scheme for Construction Contracts –

'claim by the payee' means a written notice given by the party carrying out work under a construction contract to the other party specifying the amount of any payment or payments which he considers to be due and the basis on which it is, or they are calculated;

'contract price' means the entire sum payable under the construction contract in respect of the work;

'relevant construction contract' means any construction contract other than one –

(a) which specifies that the duration of the work is to be less than 45 days, or
(b) in respect of which the parties agree that the duration of the work is estimated to be less than 45 days;

'relevant period' means a period which is specified in, or is calculated by reference to the constructon contract or where no such period is so specified or is so calculable, a period of 28 days;

'value of work' means an amount determined in accordance with the construction contract under which the work is performed or where the contract contains no such provision, the cost of any work performed in accordance with that contract together with an amount equal to any overhead or profit included in the contract price;

'work' means any of the work or services mentioned in section 104 of the Act.

# ARBITRATION ACT 1996, s 42

[. . .]

*Powers of the court in relation to arbitral proceedings*

**42   Enforcement of peremptory orders of tribunal**

(1) Unless otherwise agreed by the parties, the court may make an order requiring a party to comply with a peremptory order made by the tribunal.[1]

(2) An application for an order under this section may be made –

   (a) by the tribunal[1] (upon notice to the parties),

   (b) by a party to the arbitral proceedings[2] with the permission of the tribunal[1] (and upon notice to the other parties), or

   (c) [3].

(3) [3].

(4) No order shall be made under this section unless the court is satisfied that the person to whom the tribunal's order was directed has failed to comply with it within the time prescribed in the order or, if no time was prescribed, within a reasonable time.

(5) The leave of the court is required for any appeal from a decision of the court under this section.

---

1    Tribunal should be read as adjudicator (Sch, Pt I, para 24(a) of the Scheme for Construction Contracts (England and Wales) Regulations 1998, SI 1998/649.

2    Arbitral proceedings should be read as adjudication (ibid, para 24(b)).

3    Deletions are consequent upon ibid, para 24(c) and (d).

# Appendix 2

## THE LATHAM REPORT

### CONSTRUCTING THE TEAM

### CHAPTER NINE

### DISPUTE RESOLUTION

**9.1** 'During the past 50 years much of the United States construction environment has been degraded from one of a positive relationship between all members of the project team to a contest consumed in fault finding and defensiveness which results in litigation. The industry has become extremely adversarial and we are paying the price . . . If the construction industry is to become less adversarial, we must reexamine the construction process, particularly the relationship between contractor/subcontractor. A positive alliance of these parties constitutes an indispensable link to a successful project . . . Disputes will continue as long as people fail to trust one another.' (Newsletter from 'The Dispute Avoidance and Resolution Task Force', (Dart), Washington D.C., February 1994.)

**9.2** The UK construction industry is not alone in having adversarial attitudes. But the United States has taken positive steps to try to reduce them, with the growth of Alternative Dispute Resolution (ADR). The debate over adjudication, conciliation/mediation and arbitration has been very strong throughout this Review. There has been growing consensus over the action needed.

**9.3** The best solution is to avoid disputes. If procedures relating to procurement and tendering are improved, the causes of conflict will be reduced. If a contract document is adopted which places the emphasis on teamwork and partnership to solve problems, that is another major step. The prepricing of variations is also important.

### ADJUDICATION

**9.4** Nevertheless disputes may arise, despite everyone's best efforts to avoid them. A contract form with a built in adjudication process provides a clear route.[1] If a dispute cannot be resolved first by the parties themselves in good faith, it is referred to the adjudicator for decision. Such a system must become the key to settling disputes in the construction industry. Separate adjudication is not currently provided for within JCT 80. The architect has the specific role of contract administrator there and is under a professional duty to act impartially as between employer and contractor. This was considered at length by a working party which reported to the Joint Contracts Tribunal in 1993. It made proposals for clauses in the contract providing for mediation and/or adjudication. It spelt out how those clauses should work, and what form of disputes they should include. Other than lack of agreement within the JCT, there has been nothing to prevent the introduction of such procedures within JCT 80 already.

---

1    The SEACC system contains a particularly good model for adjudication. The Interim Report set out in detail those other contracts which have adjudication or conciliation. There is also some provision within subcontract forms.

**9.5** If the NEC becomes normal construction contract documentation, its procedures for adjudication will be followed, though they may require some amendments. But adjudication should be incorporated forthwith within the JCT family as a whole. (Regarding the JCT Minor Works Form, under which work tends to be fairly quickly carried out, the Tribunal may prefer to incorporate a similar conciliation procedure to that in the ICE Minor Works Form, though there is no inherent reason why adjudication should not be used for any size of contract.) There should be no restriction on the issues to be placed before the adjudicator for decision, and no specified 'cooling off period' before the adjudicator can be called in. The adjudicator should be named in the contract before work starts but called in when necessary.[1] The adjudicator must be neutral. If agreement cannot be reached by the parties themselves on a name, or names,[2] an appointment should be made by the Presidents of one of the appropriate professional bodies. Either party to a dispute should have the right to ask for adjudication. As well as dealing with disputes between clients and main contractors, the contract documents must specify that the adjudicator must have equal scope to determine disputes between contractors and subcontractors, and between subcontractors and sub subcontractors. Jurisdiction on subcontract issues should not be limited to disputes over set off. It should encompass any matter which can also be within the scope of resolution under the main contract. (In many cases, disputes between clients and main contractors also involve subcontractors.) The adjudicator's fee should initially be the responsibility of the party calling in the adjudicator, but the adjudicator should subsequently apportion it as appropriate. Both main contractors and subcontractors have pressed hard for such a system to be standard procedure for dispute resolution. They should now seek to make it effective, in a spirit of teamwork.

**9.6** It is crucial that adjudication decisions should be implemented at once. Mr Roger Knowles, Chairman of James R Knowles, Construction Contracts Consultants, writes: 'A well drafted disputes procedure involving adjudicators and arbitrators operating in an unrestricted manner will help disputes to be resolved quickly and inexpensively. For disputes settled by these methods, appeals and reference to the High Court should not be permitted under any circumstances, as it is the constant spectre of appeal which conditions the manner in which many arbitrations are conducted and which has emasculated the whole process'. (Paper by Mr Knowles, April 1994.)

**9.7** I have considered this proposal. It has also been made by others, who have drawn specific attention to the role of the expert under IChemE conditions. It is correct that the authority of the adjudicator/expert must be upheld, and that the decisions should be implemented at once. Such published experience as exists of adjudication – and it does not seem very extensive at main contract level, because the possibility of the system being used appears to induce the parties to reach their own settlement without recourse to it – suggests that it is successful in reducing disputes without further appeal or litigation.[3] But it would be difficult to deny a party which feels totally aggrieved by an adjudicator's decision any

---

1    Some evidence suggested that for small and medium-sized contracts there is no need to name an adjudicator in advance, but the contract document must provide for a method of appointing one if the need arises. (This suggestion is made in the Building Structures Group's final report to the Review.) On balance, I believe it would be better if the adjudicator was named even for the smallest contract, but, if not, the provisions must allow for a nominee to be appointed immediately on request. It would be damaging if the appointment of the adjudicator was frustrated by delay or disagreement by one of the parties to the dispute.

2    Medium or large sized projects may require more than one name for different areas of possible dispute. Alternatively, a multi-disciplinary firm or firms could be named.

3    See for example the article by Mr Michael Morris in the February edition of the *Journal of the Institute of Arbitrators* about Adjudication Procedures on the Dartford River Crossing, and 'Adjudicators, Experts and Keeping Out of Court' by Mr Mark C. McGraw of Lovell, White, Durrant which appeared in *Construction Law Journal*, 1992.

opportunity to appeal either to the courts or arbitration. I doubt whether such a restriction would be enforceable. The SEACC system, which generally defers access to the courts until after acceptance, allows such an earlier reference to the courts in certain specified and limited circumstances. However:

1. The adjudication result must be implemented at once, even if it is subsequently overturned by the courts or an arbitrator after practical completion. If the award of the adjudicator involves payment, it must be made at once. Placing the money in the hands of an impartial stakeholder should only be permitted with the specific agreement of all the parties in the dispute, or if the adjudicator (exceptionally) so directs.
2. The courts (unless there is some exceptional and immediate issue of law which must be brought in front of a Judge/Official Referee at once) should only be approached as a last resort and after practical completion of the contract.

## CONCILIATION AND MEDIATION

**9.8** Mediation/conciliation is another route of Alternative Dispute Resolution. It is a voluntary, non-binding process, intended to bring the parties to agreement. A mediator has no powers of enforcement or of making a binding recommendation. Some contracts which contain a conciliation[1] procedure seem to work well – the ICE Minor Works Contract is its best selling document with 'many satisfied customers'.[2] Mediation/conciliation should contain two crucial provisions.

1. The scope of the conciliation must cover all potential aspects of dispute, and that scope must be fully stepped down into subcontracts.
2. It must also be a condition of contract that such provisions are fully available to both main contractor and subcontractors without deletion, amendment or restriction.

Most disputes on site are, I believe, better resolved by speedy decision – i.e. adjudication – rather than by a mediation procedure in which the parties reach their own settlement.

## MULTI-TIERED ADR

**9.9** Some very large projects may require more than one form of dispute resolution. That section of the Hong Kong Airport Core Programme which is the Government's responsibility (basically the infrastructure and related projects) has a four tier level of dispute resolution – engineer's decision, mandatory mediation/conciliation, adjudication and arbitration.[3] It is to be hoped that such complex procedures would only be required to be used rarely. But it is proper that they should be available in such massive contracts, and special conditions attached to the form of contract could accommodate them. Some have suggested that it would be appropriate that the adjudicator should be a 3 person board for large projects, with one representative from each side of the dispute, and an independent chairperson. Such a board would need to be differently constructed if the dispute was between client and contractor than if it was between contractor and subcontractor, let alone a dispute between client and contractor to which subcontractors were joined. My view is that the board should all be independent, and a panel of names should be in the contract to deal with all major disputes. Dispute review boards have proved successful in the United States.

---

1 The CIEC report says that the ICE Conciliation Procedure is currently being revised to place more emphasis on reaching an agreed solution.
2 Source: Letter from Mr Guy Cottam, February 1994.
3 The airport itself has a two tier procedure – decision of the project director and arbitration. The airport railway has engineer's decison, mediation and arbitration. (Source: Masons, providing a paper by Mr Michael Byrne of the Government secretariat.)

## ARBITRATION

**9.10** Arbitrators are an expert and dedicated group of people, with whom I have had constructive discussions during the Review. Many of them also serve now as conciliators or experts, and in other forms of Alternative Dispute Resolution, and they may form a core resource for the adjudication system. As stated in the Interim Report, there is considerable dissatisfaction with arbitration within the construction industry because of its perceived complexity, slowness and expense. The arbitrators themselves favour reforms to the procedures which will allow for less formality and speedier hearings.[1] Following the report of a Committee under the chairmanship of Lord Justice Steyn, the Department of Trade & Industry has published a draft Bill and consultation paper which seeks to clarify and consolidate the law (February 1994). Arbitration has a continuing part to play in dispute resolution within the construction industry. But it should be a last resort after practical completion, if a party to a dispute remains aggrieved by the decision of the adjudicator even though that decision has already been implemented. If the proposed system of adjudication works properly, many current arbitrators will be making decisions during the course of the project, but in the role of adjudicators, which is what many of them would wish to be able to do now. There are provisions for speedy arbitration hearings during the course of the contract under rule 7 of the JCT Arbitration Rules 1988. But the experience of arbitrators themselves is that they are little used. Full arbitration after the completion of the contract will, hopefully, become much rarer.

## INTERIM PAYMENTS, ADJUDICATION AND THE COURTS

**9.11** Concern has also been expressed to me about the operation of Supreme Court Rules 14 and 29 relating to Summary Judgment or interim payment of awards. The Official Referees Solicitors Association (ORSA) has made proposals about interim payments:

1.   The amount of any interim payment should be the court's best estimate at that stage of the amount for which the plaintiff would succeed, taking account of any serious cross claims by the defendant which might be sustained.
2.   If the court is unable to make an adequate estimate, it could refer the matter for report by a Court Adjudicator, whose recommendation would normally be accepted.

(Source: Discussion Paper by ORSA, 'Interim Payment Awards in Building Contract Cases', July 1992.)

**9.12** The draft Arbitration Bill published by the DTI also contains, in clause 14, proposals for possible interim payments. However, the wording of subclause (1) requires the arbitrator (or 'tribunal') to be 'satisfied' that the respondent will be found liable to pay to the claimant a sum at least equal to the amount of the interim payment. If the arbitrator acts in practice as the courts have done over RSC Orders 14 and 29, the likelihood is that few such awards would be made. Clause 14(3) of the draft Bill would also allow the parties to omit such provisions by agreement. The commercial dominance of some parties in construction contracts suggests that it is better not to have clauses which 'allow' participants to opt out of fair dispute resolution procedures.

**9.13** Recourse to the courts or arbitration should become less frequent because of other changes which I have recommended to procurement practice, contract conditions, tighter restrictions over set-off and the introduction of adjudicators as a normal procedure for settling disputes. The detailed working of the Courts of Justice, of which the Official Referees are a distinguished part, is not a matter on which I feel competent to make recommendations. Very

---

1    *Evidence by the Chartered Institute of Arbitrators*, January 1994.

senior judges have stressed that holding up the flow of cash is bad for the construction industry.[1] If adjudication is introduced as the normal method of dispute resolution in construction, the courts will perhaps take account of the wishes of the industry to ensure that cash does flow speedily. But one regrettable possibility could be if a party to an adjudication refused to honour the award of the adjudicator immediately, or even to discuss the use of stake holders, despite being bound to do so. In such circumstances, the party to whom the award had been made should be able to approach the Official Referee immediately and obtain a judgment for payment under an expedited procedure as suggested by ORSA, be it under Rules 14 or 29, or any other appropriate legal provision. It would be fatal to the adjudication system if one party successfully attempted to use greater financial strength to exhaust the other by delays in settlement. The courts should have a role to support the adjudication system in such circumstances.

## RECOMMENDATIONS 26.1–26.5: ADJUDICATION

**9.14** I have already recommended that a system of adjudication should be introduced within all the Standard Forms of Contract (except where comparable arrangements already exist for mediation or conciliation) and that this should be underpinned by legislation. I also recommend that:

1.   There should be no restrictions on the issues capable of being referred to the adjudicator, conciliator or mediator, either in the main contract or subcontract documentation.
2.   The award of the adjudicator should be implemented immediately. The use of stake holders should only be permitted if both parties agree or if the adjudicator so directs.
3.   Any appeals to arbitration or the courts should be after practical completion, and should not be permitted to delay the implementation of the award, unless an immediate and exceptional issue arises for the courts or as in the circumstances described in (4) below.
4.   Resort to the courts should be immediately available if a party refuses to implement the award of an adjudicator. In such circumstances, the courts may wish to support the system of adjudication by agreeing to expedited procedures for interim payments.
5.   Training procedures should be devised for adjudicators. A Code of Practice should also be drawn up under the auspices of the proposed Implementation Forum.

---

1   Cf Lord Justice Lawton 'The Courts are aware of what happens in these building disputes; cases go either to arbitration or before an Official Referee; they drag on and on; the cash flow is held up ... that sort of result is to be avoided if possible' (*Ellis Mechanical Services v Wates Construction Limited* (1976) 2 BLR 57).

# Appendix 3

## ADJUDICATION SCHEMES

### Contents

# THE TECHNOLOGY AND CONSTRUCTION SOLICITORS ASSOCIATION TeCSA ADJUDICATION RULES – 1999 VERSION 1.3 PROCEDURAL RULES FOR ADJUDICATION

1. The following rules

(i) may be incorporated into any contract by reference to the 'TeCSA Adjudication Rules' or the 'ORSA Adjudication Rules', which expressions shall mean, in relation to any adjudication, the most recent edition hereof as at the date of the written notice requiring that adjudication.

(ii) meet the requirements of adjudication procedure as set out in section 108 of the Housing Grants, Construction and Regeneration Act 1996; Part I of the Scheme for Construction Contracts shall thus not apply.

## DEFINITIONS

2. In these Rules:

'Contract' means the agreement which includes the agreement to adjudicate in accordance with these Rules

'Party' means any party to the Contract

'Chairman' means the Chairman for the time being of the Technology and Construction Solicitors Association ('TeCSA'), or such other officer thereof as is authorised to deputise for him.

## COMMENCEMENT

3(i) These Rules shall apply upon any Party giving written notice to any other Party requiring adjudication, and identifying in general terms the dispute in respect of which adjudication is required.

(ii) Within 7 days from the date of such notice, and provided that he is willing and able to act, any agreed Adjudicator under Rule 6 or nominated Adjudicator under Rule 7(ii) or replacement Adjudicator under Rule 8 shall give written notice of his acceptance of appointment to all parties.

(iii) The date of the referral of the dispute shall be the date that the Adjudicator so confirms his acceptance.

4. Notice requiring adjudication may be given at any time and notwithstanding that arbitration or litigation has been commenced in respect of such dispute.

5. More than one such notice requiring adjudication may be given arising out of the same contract.

## APPOINTMENT

6. Where the Parties have agreed upon the identity of an adjudicator who confirms his readiness and willingness to embark upon the Adjudication within 7 days of the notice requiring adjudication, then that person shall be the Adjudicator.

7. Where the Parties have not so agreed upon an adjudicator, or where such person has not so confirmed his willingness to act, then any Party may apply to the Chairman of TeCSA for a nomination. The following procedure shall apply:

(i) The application shall be in writing, accompanied by a copy of the Contract or other evidence of the agreement of the Parties that these Rules should apply, a copy of the written notice requiring adjudication, and TeCSA's appointment fee of £100.

(ii) The Chairman of TeCSA shall endeavour to secure the appointment of an Adjudicator and the referral to him of the dispute within 7 days from the notice requiring adjudication.

(iii) Any person so appointed, and not any person named in the Contract whose readiness or willingness is in question, shall be the Adjudicator.

8. The Chairman of TeCSA shall have the power by written notice to the Parties to replace the Adjudicator with another nominated person if and when it appears necessary to him to do so. The Chairman of TeCSA shall consider whether to exercise such power if any Party shall represent to him that the Adjudicator is not acting impartially, or that the Adjudicator is physically or mentally incapable of conducting the Adjudication, or that the Adjudicator is failing with necessary dispatch to proceed with the Adjudication or

make his decision. In the event of a replacement under this Rule, directions and decisions of the previous Adjudicator shall remain in effect unless reviewed and replaced by the new Adjudicator, and all timescales shall be recalculated from the date of the replacement.

9. Where an Adjudicator has already been appointed in relation to another dispute arising out of the Contract, the Chairman of TeCSA may appoint either the same or a different person as Adjudicator.

## AGREEMENT

10. An agreement to adjudicate in accordance with these Rules shall be treated as an offer made by each of the Parties to TeCSA and to any Adjudicator to abide by these Rules, which offer may be accepted by conduct by appointing an Adjudicator or embarking upon the Adjudication respectively.

## SCOPE OF THE ADJUDICATION

11. The scope of the Adjudication shall be the matters identified in the notice requiring adjudication, together with

(i) any further matters which all Parties agree should be within the scope of the Adjudication, and
(ii) any further matters which the Adjudicator determines must be included in order that the adjudication may be effective and/or meaningful.

12. The Adjudicator may rule upon his own substantive jurisdiction, and as to the scope of the Adjudication.

## THE PURPOSE OF THE ADJUDICATION AND THE ROLE OF THE ADJUDICATOR

13. The underlying purpose of the Adjudication is to resolve disputes between the Parties that are within the scope of the Adjudication as rapidly and economically as is reasonably possible.

14. Decisions of the Adjudicator shall be binding until the dispute is finally determined by legal proceedings, by arbitration (if the Contract provides for arbitration or the parties otherwise agree to arbitration) or by agreement.

15. Wherever possible, the decision of the Adjudicator shall reflect the legal entitlements of the Parties. Where it appears to the Adjudicator impossible to reach a concluded view upon the legal entitlements of the Parties within the practical constraints of a rapid and economical adjudication process, his decision shall represent his fair and reasonable view, in light of the facts and the law insofar as they have been ascertained by the Adjudicator, of how the disputed matter should lie unless and until resolved by litigation or arbitration.

16. The Adjudicator shall have the like power to open up and review any certificates or other things issued or made pursuant to the Contract as would an arbitrator appointed pursuant to the Contract and/or a court.

17. The Adjudicator shall act fairly and impartially, but shall not be obliged or empowered to act as though he were an arbitrator.

## CONDUCT OF THE ADJUDICATION

18. The Adjudicator shall establish the procedure and timetable for the Adjudication.

19. Without prejudice to the generality of Rule 18, the Adjudicator may if he thinks fit:

(i) Require the delivery of written statements of case,
(ii) Require any party to produce a bundle of key documents, whether helpful or otherwise to that Party's case, and to draw such inference as may seem proper from any imbalance in such bundle that may become apparent,
(iii) Require the delivery to him and/or the other parties of copies of any documents other than documents that would be privileged from production to a court,
(iv) Limit the length of any written or oral submission,
(v) Require the attendance before him for questioning of any Party or employee or agent of any Party,
(vi) Make site visits,
(vii) Make use of his own specialist knowledge,

(viii) Obtain advice from specialist consultants, provided that at least one of the Parties so requests or consents,

(ix) Meet and otherwise communicate with any Party without the presence of other Parties,

(x) Make directions for the conduct of the Adjudication orally or in writing,

(xi) Review and revise any of his own previous directions,

(xii) Conduct the Adjudication inquisitorially, and take the initiative in ascertaining the facts and the law,

(xiii) Reach his decision with or without holding an oral hearing, and with or without having endeavoured to facilitate an agreement between the Parties.

20. The Adjudicator shall exercise such powers with a view of fairness and impartiality, giving each Party a reasonable opportunity, in light of the timetable, of putting his case and dealing with that of his opponents.

21. The Adjudicator may not:

(i) Require any advance payment of or security for his fees,

(ii) Receive any written submissions from one Party that are not also made available to the others,

(iii) Refuse any Party the right at any hearing or meeting to be represented by any representative of that Party's choosing who is present,

(iv) Act or continue to act in the face of a conflict of interest,

(v) Require any Party to pay or make contribution to the legal costs of another Party arising in the Adjudication.

22. The Adjudicator shall reach a decision within 28 days of referral or such longer period as is agreed by the Parties after the dispute has been referred to him. The Adjudicator shall be entitled to extend the said period of 28 days by up to 14 days with the consent of the Party by whom the dispute was referred.

## ADJUDICATOR'S FEES AND EXPENSES

23. If a Party shall request Adjudication, and it is subsequently established that he is not entitled to do so, that Party shall be solely responsible for the Adjudicator's fees and expenses.

24. Save as aforesaid, the Parties shall be jointly responsible for the Adjudicator's fees and expenses including those of any specialist consultant appointed under 19(viii). In his decision, the Adjudicator shall have the discretion to make directions with regard to those fees and expenses. If no such directions are made, the Parties shall bear such fees and expenses in equal shares, and if any Party has paid more than such equal share, that Party shall be entitled to contribution from other Parties accordingly.

25. The Adjudicator's fees shall not exceed the rate of £1000 per day or part day, plus expenses and VAT.

## DECISIONS

26. The Adjudicator may in any decision direct the payment of such compound or simple interest as may be commercially reasonable.

27. All decisions shall be in writing, but shall not include any reasons.

## ENFORCEMENT

28. Every decision of the Adjudicator shall be implemented without delay. The Parties shall be entitled to such reliefs and remedies as are set out in the decision, and shall be entitled to summary enforcement thereof, regardless of whether such decision is or is to be the subject of any challenge or review. No party shall be entitled to raise any right of set-off, counterclaim or abatement in connection with any enforcement proceedings.

## IMMUNITY, CONFIDENTIALITY AND NON-COMPELLABILITY

29. Neither TeCSA, nor its Chairman, nor deputy, nor the Adjudicator nor any employee or agent of any of them shall be liable for anything done or not done in the discharge or purported discharge of his functions as Adjudicator, whether in negligence or otherwise, unless the act or omission is in bad faith.

30. The Adjudication and all matters arising in the course thereof are and will be kept confidential by the Parties except insofar as necessary to implement or enforce any decision of the Adjudicator or as may be required for the purpose of any subsequent proceedings.

31. In the event that any Party seeks to challenge or review any decision of the Adjudicator in any subsequent litigation or arbitration, the Adjudicator shall not be joined as a party to, nor shall be subpoenaed or otherwise required to give evidence or provide his notes in such litigation or arbitration.

## LAW

32. These Rules shall be governed by English law and under the jurisdiction of the English Courts.

33. No Party shall, save in case of bad faith on the part of the Adjudicator, make any application to the courts whatsoever in relation to the conduct of the Adjudication or the decision of the Adjudicator until such time as the Adjudicator has made his decision, or refused to make a decision, and until the Party making the application has complied with any such decision.

January 1999

## NOTES

*These notes do not form part of the TeCSA Adjudication Rules*

These rules are designed to meet the requirements for adjudication set out at Part II of the Housing Grants, Construction and Regeneration Act 1996. They may be incorporated into contracts, including contracts contained in correspondence, by suitable wording along the following lines:

Any dispute arising under this agreement shall in the first instance be referred to adjudication in accordance with the TeCSA Adjudication Rules.

This Version 1.3 is substantially the same as Version 1.2 of these rules issued under TeCSA's former name: The Official Referees' Solicitors Association. In order to prevent the need for re-drafting or recalling Contracts, Rule 1(i) now provides that these Rules may be incorporated by reference either to the 'TeCSA Adjudication Rules' or the 'ORSA Adjudication Rules'.

The Housing Grants, Construction and Regeneration Act 1996 gives parties to a construction contract other than with a residential occupier or an excluded contract entered into after 1st May 1998 a right to refer a dispute arising under the contract to adjudication. If the contract does not incorporate the TeCSA Adjudication Rules or other provisions meeting the compliance criteria set out in the Act, then the terms of Part I of the Scheme for Construction Contracts become applicable.

If the contract does not incorporate the TeCSA Adjudication rules or otherwise comply with the compliance criteria such that there is no agreed adjudication or nominating body, then a disputant may yet ask TeCSA to appoint an adjudicator; TeCSA is an 'adjudicator nominating body' within the meaning of paragraph 2(3) of The Scheme for Construction Contracts (England and Wales) Regulations 1998. An adjudicator so appointed will conduct the adjudication in accordance with the Scheme, or if the parties so agree, the TeCSA Adjudication Rules.

If the contract contains an arbitration clause, then in order to prevent enforcement difficulties arising out of Section 9 of the Arbitration Act 1996, TeCSA recommends that the arbitration clause should contain wording along the following lines:

Provided always that the enforcement of any decision of an adjudicator is not a matter which may be referred to arbitration.

Applications to the Chairman of TeCSA should be addressed to:

Robert Fenwick Elliott Esq
Technology and Construction Solicitors Association
353 Strand
London WC2R 0HS
Tel: 0171 956 9354
Fax: 0171 956 9355/64
email: rjfe@fenwickelliott.co.uk

*TeCSA and its members take no responsibility for loss or damage caused to any user of these Rules or these Notes.*

# THE INSTITUTION OF CIVIL ENGINEERS' (ICE) ADJUDICATION PROCEDURE 1997

## 1. GENERAL PRINCIPLES

1.1 The adjudication shall be conducted in accordance with the edition of the ICE Adjudication Procedure which is current at the date of issue of a notice in writing of intention to refer a dispute to adjudication (hereinafter called the Notice of Adjudication) and the Adjudicator shall be appointed under the Adjudicator's Agreement which forms a part of this Procedure. If a conflict arises between this Procedure and the Contract then this Procedure shall prevail.

1.2 The object of adjudication is to reach a fair, rapid and inexpensive determination of a dispute arising under the Contract and this Procedure shall be interpreted accordingly.

1.3 The Adjudicator shall be a named individual and shall act impartially.

1.4 In making a decision, the Adjudicator may take the initiative in ascertaining the facts and the law. The adjudication shall be neither an expert determination nor an arbitration but the Adjudicator may rely on his own expert knowledge and experience.

1.5 The Adjudicator's decision shall be binding until the dispute is finally determined by legal proceedings, by arbitration (if the Contract provides for arbitration or the Parties otherwise agree to arbitration) or by agreement.

1.6 The Parties shall implement the Adjudicator's decision without delay whether or not the dispute is to be referred to legal proceedings or arbitration. Payment shall be made in accordance with the payment provisions in the Contract, in the next stage payment which becomes due after the date of issue of the decision, unless otherwise directed by the Adjudicator unless the decision is in relation to an effective notice under Section 111 of the Act.

## 2. THE NOTICE OF ADJUDICATION

2.1 Any Party may give notice at any time of its intention to refer a dispute arising under the Contract to adjudication by giving a written Notice of Adjudication to the other Party. The Notice of Adjudication shall include:

(a) the details and date of the Contract between the Parties;
(b) the issues which the Adjudicator is being asked to decide;
(c) details of the nature and extent of the redress sought.

## 3. THE APPOINTMENT OF THE ADJUDICATOR

3.1 When an Adjudicator has either been named in the Contract or agreed prior to the issue of the Notice of Adjudication the Party issuing the Notice of Adjudication shall at the same time send to the Adjudicator a copy of the Notice of Adjudication and a request for confirmation, within four days of the date of issue of the Notice of Adjudication, that the Adjudicator is able and willing to act.

3.2 When an Adjudicator has not been so named or agreed the Party issuing the Notice of Adjudication may include with the Notice the names of one or more persons with their addresses who have agreed to act, any one of whom would be acceptable to the referring Party, for selection by the other Party. The other Party shall select and notify the referring Party and the selected Adjudicator within four days of the date of issue of the Notice of Adjudication.

3.3 If confirmation is not received under paragraph 3.1 or a selection is not made under paragraph 3.2 or the Adjudicator does not accept or is unable to act then either Party may within a further three days request the person or body named in the Contract or if none is so named The Institution of Civil Engineers to appoint the Adjudicator. Such request shall be in writing on the appropriate form of application for the appointment of an adjudicator and accompanied by a copy of the Notice of Adjudication and the appropriate fee.

3.4 The Adjudicator shall be appointed on the terms and conditions set out in the attached Adjudicator's Agreement and Schedule and shall be entitled to be paid a reasonable fee together with his expenses. The Parties shall sign the agreement within 7 days of being requested to do so.

3.5 If for any reason whatsoever the Adjudicator is unable to act, either Party may require the appointment of a replacement adjudicator in accordance with the procedure in paragraph 3.3.

## 4. REFERRAL

4.1 The referring Party shall within two days of receipt of confirmation under 3.1, or notification of selection under 3.2, or appointment under 3.3 send to the Adjudicator, with a copy to the other Party, a full statement of his case which should include:

(a) a copy of the Notice of Adjudication;
(b) a copy of any adjudication provision in the Contract, and
(c) the information upon which he relies, including supporting documents.

4.2 The date of referral of the dispute to adjudication shall be the date upon which the Adjudicator receives the documents referred to in paragraph 4.1.

## 5. CONDUCT OF THE ADJUDICATION

5.1 The Adjudicator shall reach his decision within 28 days of referral, or such longer period as is agreed by the Parties after the dispute has been referred. The period of 28 days may be extended by up to 14 days with the consent of the referring Party.

5.2 The Adjudicator shall determine the matters set out in the Notice of Adjudication, together with any other matters which the Parties and the Adjudicator agree should be within the scope of the adjudication.

5.3 The Adjudicator may open up review and revise any decision, (other than that of an adjudicator unless agreed by the Parties), opinion, instruction, direction, certificate or valuation made under or in connection with the Contract and to which the dispute relates to determine the rights and obligations of the Parties. He may order the payment of a sum of money, or other redress but no decision of the Adjudicator shall affect the freedom of the Parties to vary the terms of the Contract or the Engineer to vary the works in accordance with the Contract.

5.4 The other Party may submit his response to the statement under paragraph 4.1 within 14 days of referral. The period of response may be extended by agreement between the Parties and the Adjudicator.

5.5 The Adjudicator shall have complete discretion as to how to conduct the adjudication, and shall establish the procedure and timetable, subject to any limitation that there may be in the Contract or the Act. He shall not be required to observe any rule of evidence, procedure or otherwise, of any court. Without prejudice to the generality of these powers, he may:

(a) ask for further written information;

  (b)  meet and question the Parties and their representatives;

  (c)  visit the site;

  (d)  request the production of documents or the attendance of people whom he considers could assist;

  (e)  set times for (a)–(d) and similar activities;

  (f)  proceed with the adjudication and reach a decision even if a Party fails:

     (i)  to provide information;

     (ii)  to attend a meeting;

     (iii)  to take any other action requested by the Adjudicator;

  (g)  issue such further directions as he considers to be appropriate.

5.6 The Adjudicator may obtain legal or technical advice having first notified the Parties of his intention.

5.7 Any Party may at any time ask that additional Parties shall be joined in the adjudication. Joinder of additional Parties shall be subject to the agreement of the Adjudicator and the existing and additional Parties. An additional Party shall have the same rights and obligations as the other Parties, unless otherwise agreed by the Adjudicator and the Parties.

# 6. THE DECISION

6.1 The Adjudicator shall reach his decision and so notify the Parties within the time limits in paragraph 5.1 and may reach a decision on different aspects of the dispute at different times. He shall not be required to give reasons.

6.2 The Adjudicator may in any decision direct the payment of such simple or compound interest at such rate and between such dates or such events as he considers appropriate.

6.3 Should the Adjudicator fail to reach his decision and notify the Parties in the due time either Party may give seven days' notice of its intention to refer the dispute to a replacement adjudicator appointed in accordance with the procedures in paragraph 3.3.

6.4 If the Adjudicator fails to reach and notify his decision in due time the decision shall still be effective if it is notified before the referral of the dispute to a replacement adjudicator under paragrah 6.3.

If the Parties are so notified after the dispute has been referred to a replacement adjudicator then the decision shall be of no effect and the Adjudicator shall not be entitled to any fees or expenses but the Parties shall be responsible for the fees and expenses of any legal or technical adviser appointed under paragraph 5.6 subject to the Parties having received such advice.

6.5 The Parties shall bear their own costs and expenses incurred in the adjudication. The Parties shall be jointly and severally responsible for the Adjudicator's fees and expenses, including those of any legal or technical adviser appointed under paragraph 5.6, but in his decision the Adjudicator may direct a Party to pay all or part of his fees and expenses. If he makes no such direction the Parties shall pay them in equal shares.

6.6 At any time until 7 days before the Adjudicator is due to reach his decision, he may give notice to the Parties that he will deliver it only on full payment of his fees and expenses. Any Party may then pay these costs in order to obtain the decision and recover the other Party's share of the costs in accordance with paragraph 6.5 as a debt due.

6.7 The Parties shall be entitled to the relief and remedies set out in the decision and to seek summary enforcement thereof, regardless of whether the dispute is to be referred to legal proceedings or arbitration. No issue decided by an adjudicator may subsequently be laid before another adjudicator unless so agreed by the Parties.

6.8  In the event that the dispute is referred to legal proceedings or arbitration, the Adjudicator's decision shall not inhibit the court or arbitrator from determining the Parties' rights or obligations anew.

6.9  The Adjudicator may on his own initiative, or on the request of either Party, correct a decision so as to remove any clerical mistake, error or ambiguity provided that the initiative is taken, or the request is made within 14 days of the notification of the decision to the Parties. The Adjudicator shall make his corrections within 7 days of any request by a Party.

## 7. MISCELLANEOUS PROVISIONS

7.1  Unless the Parties agree, the Adjudicator shall not be appointed arbitrator in any subsequent arbitration between the Parties under the Contract. No Party may call the Adjudicator as a witness in any legal proceedings or arbitration concerning the subject matter of the adjudication.

7.2  The Adjudicator shall not be liable for anything done or omitted in the discharge or purported discharge of his functions as Adjudicator unless the act or omission is in bad faith, and any employee or agent of the Adjudicator shall be similarly protected from liability. The Parties shall save harmless and indemnify the Adjudicator and any employee or agent of the Adjudicator against all claims by third parties and in respect of this shall be jointly and severally liable.

7.3  Neither The Institution of Civil Engineers (or any other adjudication nomination body or person named in the Contract or selected by a Party to nominate or appoint an adjudicator) nor its servants or agents shall be liable to any Party for any act omission or misconduct in connection with any appointment made or any adjudication conducted under this Procedure.

7.4  All notices shall be sent by recorded delivery to the address stated in the Contract for service of notices, or if none, the principal place of business or registered office (in the case of a company). Any agreement required by this Procedure shall be evidenced in writing.

7.5  This Procedure shall be interpreted in accordance with the law of the Contract.

## 8. DEFINITIONS

8.1  (a)  The 'Act' means the Housing Grants, Construction and Regeneration Act 1996.
　　(b)  The 'Adjudicator' means the person named as such in the Contract or appointed in accordance with this Procedure.
　　(c)  'Contract' means the contract or the agreement between the Parties which contains the provision for adjudication.
　　(d)  'Party' means a Party to the Contract and references to either Party or the other Party or Parties shall include any additional Party or Parties joined in accordance with this Procedure.

## 9. APPLICATION TO PARTICULAR CONTRACTS

9.1  When this Procedure is used with The Institution of Civil Engineers' Agreement for Consultancy Work in Respect of Domestic or Small Works the Adjudicator may determine any dispute in connection with or arising out of the Contract.

9.2  Notwithstanding the provisions in paragraphs 1.1, 1.2 and 2.1 where the jurisdiction of the Adjudicator described in the Contract differs from that described in this Procedure then the Contract shall prevail.

*A copy of the appropriate form for applying for an appointment by The Institution of Civil Engineers may be obtained from:*

The Dispute Administration Service, The Institution of Civil Engineers, 1 Great George Street, Westminster, LONDON SW1P 3AA

Telephone: +44 (0)171 222 7722 Facsimile: +44 (0)171 222 1403

# ADJUDICATOR'S AGREEMENT

THIS AGREEMENT is made on the                    day of                    19

between (the first Party):

of:

and (the second Party):

of:

and (where there is a third Party):

of:

(hereinafter called 'the Parties') of the one part and:

of:

(hereinafter called 'the Adjudicator') of the other part.

Disputes or differences may arise/have arisen* between the Parties under or in connection with a Contract dated                    and

known as:

and these disputes or differences shall be/have been* referred to adjudication in accordance with The Institution of Civil Engineers' Adjudication Procedure (1997) (hereinafter called 'the Procedure') and the Adjudicator has been requested to act.

**IT IS NOW AGREED** as follows:

1.  The rights and obligations of the Adjudicator and the Parties shall be as set out in the Procedure.
2.  The Adjudicator hereby accepts the appointment and agrees to conduct the adjudication in accordance with the Procedure.
3.  The Parties bind themselves jointly and severally to pay the Adjudicator's fees and expenses in accordance with the Procedure as set out in the attached Schedule.
4.  The Parties and the Adjudicator shall at all times maintain the confidentiality of the adjudication and shall endeavour to ensure that anyone acting on their behalf or through them will do likewise, save with the consent of the other Parties which consent shall not be unreasonably refused.
5.  The Adjudicator shall inform the Parties if he intends to destroy the documents which have been sent to him in relation to the adjudication and he shall retain documents for a further period at the request of either Party.

* Delete as necessary

Signed on behalf of:

**First Party:**

Name:

Signature:

Date:

**Second Party:**

Name:

Signature:

Date:

**Third Party** (where there is a Third Party):

Name:

Signature:

Date:

**Adjudicator:**

Name:

Signature:

Date:

## SCHEDULE TO THE ADJUDICATOR'S AGREEMENT

1. The Adjudicator shall be paid at the hourly rate of £         in respect of all time spent upon, or in connection with, the adjudication including time spent travelling.
2. The Adjudicator shall be reimbursed in respect of all disbursements properly made including, but not restricted to:
   (a) Printing, reproduction and purchase of documents, drawings, maps, records and photographs.
   (b) Telegrams, telex, faxes, and telephone calls.
   (c) Postage and similar delivery charges.
   (d) Travelling, hotel expenses and other similar disbursements.
   (e) Room charges.
   (f) Charges for legal or technical advice obtained in accordance with the Procedure.
   The Adjudicator shall be paid an appointment fee of £        . This fee shall become payable in equal amounts by each Party within 14 days of the appointment of the Adjudicator. This fee will be deducted from the final statement of any sums which shall become payable under item 1 and/or item 2 of this Schedule. If the final statement is less than the appointment fee the balance shall be refunded to the Parties.
4. The Adjudicator is/is not* currently registered for VAT.
5. Where the Adjudicator is registered for VAT it shall be charged additionally in accordance with the rates current at the date of invoice.
6. All payments, other than the appointment fee (item 3) shall become due 7 days after receipt of invoice, thereafter interest shall be payable at 5% per annum above the Bank of England base rate for every day the amount remains outstanding. If the final statement is less than the appointment fee the balance is refunded to the Parties in equal amounts.

* Delete as necessary

*Source:* The Institution of Civil Engineers, *The Adjudication Procedure 1997* (Thomas Telford Limited, London, 1997)

# CONSTRUCTION INDUSTRY COUNCIL (CIC) MODEL ADJUDICATION PROCEDURE: SECOND EDITION

The Model Adjudication Procedure (MAP) forms part of the guidance, which the Construction Industry Council (CIC) is providing to assist with the implementation of the statutory right to adjudication. It is drafted to comply with section 108 of the Housing Grants, Construction and Regeneration Act and can be incorporated by reference into a contract, or used by agreement of the parties.

The MAP is for use where the law of the contract is that of England and Wales. Where the law of the contract is that of Scotland amend paragraph 30, line 2, by deleting the word 'summary' and at paragraph 35, line 2, substitute 'Scotland' for 'England and Wales'.

The MAP is accompanied by a model adjudicator agreement.

## General Principles

1. *Object*
   The object of adjudication is to reach a fair, rapid and inexpensive decision upon a dispute arising under the Contract and this procedure shall be interpreted accordingly.

2. *Impartiality*
   The Adjudicator shall act impartially.

3. *The Adjudicator's role*
   The Adjudicator may take the initiative in ascertaining the facts and the law. He may use his own knowlege and experience. The adjudication shall be neither an arbitration nor an expert determination.

4. *Decision binding in interim*
   The Adjudicator's decision shall be binding until the dispute is finally determined by legal proceedings, by arbitration (if the contract provides for arbitration or the parties otherwise agree to arbitration) or by agreement.

5. *Implementation of the decision*
   The Parties shall implement the Adjudicator's decision without delay whether or not the dispute is to be referred to legal proceedings or arbitration.

## Application

6. *Application*
   If this procedure is incorporated into the Contract by reference, the reference shall be deemed to be to the edition current at the date of the Notice.

7. *Conflict*
   If a conflict arises between this procedure and the Contract, unless the Contract provides otherwise, this procedure shall prevail.

## The Appointment of the Adjudicator

8. *Notice of adjudication*
   Either Party may give notice at any time of its intention to refer a dispute arising under the Contract to adjudication by giving a written Notice to the other Party. The Notice shall include a brief statement of the issue or issues which it is desired to refer and the redress

sought. The referring Party shall send a copy of the Notice to any adjudicator named in the Contract.

9. *Time for appointment and referral*
   The object of the procedure in paragraphs 10–14 is to secure the appointment of the Adjudicator and referral of the dispute to him within 7 days of the giving of the Notice.

10. *Appointment*
    If an adjudicator is named in the Contract, he shall within 2 days of receiving the Notice confirm his availability to act. If no adjudicator is named, or if the named adjudicator does not so confirm, the referring Party shall request the body stated in the Contract, if any, or if none the Construction Industry Council, to nominate an Adjudicator within 5 days of receipt of the request. The request shall be in writing, accompanied by a copy of the Notice and the appropriate fee. Alternatively the Parties may, within 2 days of the giving of the Notice, appoint the Adjudicator by agreement.

11. *Adjudicator unable to act*
    If, for any reason whatsoever, the Adjudicator is unble to act, or fails to reach his decision within the time required by this procedure, either Party may request the body stated in the Contract if any, or if none the Construction Industry Council, to nominate a replacement adjudicator. No such request may be made after the adjudicator has notified the Parties that he has reached his decision.

12. *Adjudicator's terms and conditions*
    Unless in the Contract provides otherwise, the Adjudicator shall be appointed on the terms and conditions set out in the attached Agreement and shall be entitled to a reasonable fee and expenses.

13. *Objection to appointment*
    If a Party objects to the appointment of a particular person as adjudicator, that objection shall not invalidate the Adjudicator's appointment or any decision he may reach.

**Conduct of the Adjudication**

14. *Statement of case*
    The referring Party shall send the Adjudicator within 7 days of the giving of the Notice (or as soon thereafter as the Adjudicator is appointed) and at the same time copy to the other Party, a statement of its case including a copy of the Notice, the Contract, details of the circumstances giving rise to the dispute, the reasons why it is entitled to the redress sought, and the evidence upon which it relies. The statement of case shall be confined to the issues raised in the Notice.

15. *Date of referral*
    The date of referral shall be the date on which the Adjudicator receives this statement of case.

16. *Period for decision*
    The Adjudicator shall reach his decision within 28 days of the date of referral, or such longer period as is agreed by the Parties after the dispute has been referred. The Adjudicator may extend the period of 28 days by up to 14 days with the consent of the referring Party.

17. *Procedure*
    The Adjudicator shall have complete discretion as to how to conduct the adjudication, and shall establish the procedure and timetable, subject to any limitation there may be in the Contract or the Act. He shall not be required to observe any rule of evidence, procedure or

otherwise, of any court or tribunal. Without prejudice to the generality of these powers, he may:

(i)     request a written defence, further argument or counter argument
(ii)    request the production of documents or the attendance of people whom he considers could assist
(iii)   visit the site
(iv)   meet and question the Parties and their representatives
(v)    meet the Parties separately
(vi)   limit the length or time for submission of any statement, defence or argument
(vii)   proceed with the adujudication and reach a decision even if a Party fails to comply with a request or direction of the Adjudicator
(viii)   issue such further directions as he considers to be appropriate.

18. *Parties to comply*
The Parties shall comply with any request or direction of the Adjudicator in relation to the adjudication.

19. *Obtaining advice*
The Adjudicator may obtain legal or technical advice, provided that he has notified the Parties of his intention first. He shall provide the Parties with copies of any written advice received.

20. *Matters to be determined*
The Adjudicator shall decide the matters set out in the Notice, together with any other matters which the Parties and the Adjudicator agree shall be within the scope of the adjudication.

21. *Adjudicator to apply the law*
The Adjudicator shall determine the rights and obligations of the Parties in accordance with the law of the Contract.

22. *Joining third parties*
Any Party may at any time ask that additional parties shall be joined in the adjudication. Joinder of additional parties shall be subject to the agreement of the Adjudicator and the existing and additional parties. An additional party shall have the same rights and obligations as the other Parties, unless otherwise agreed by the Adjudicator and the Parties.

23. *Resignation*
The Adjudicator may resign at any time on giving notice in writing to the Parties.

## The Decision

24. *Reasons*
The Adjudicator shall reach his decision within the time limits in paragraph 16. The Adjudicator may withhold delivery of his decision until his fees and expenses have been paid. He shall be required to give reasons unless both Parties agree at any time that he shall not be required to give reasons.

25. *Late decisions*
If the Adjudicator fails to reach his decision within the time permitted by this procedure, his decision shall nonetheless be effective if reached before the referral of the dispute to any replacement adjudicator under paragraph 11 but not otherwise. If he fails to reach such an effective decision, he shall not be entitled to any fees or expenses (save for the cost of any legal or technical advice subject to the Parties having received such advice).

26. *Power to open up certificates*

The Adjudicator may open up, review and revise any certificate, decision, direction, instruction, notice, opinion, requirement or valuation made in relation to the Contract.

27. *Interest*

The Adjudicator may in any decision direct the payment of such simple or compound interest from such dates, at such rates and with such rests, as he considers appropriate.

28. *Costs*

The Parties shall bear their own costs and expenses incurred in the adjudication.

29. *Adjudicator's fees and expenses*

The Parties shall be jointly and severally liable for the Adjudicator's fees and expenses, including those of any legal or technical adviser appointed under paragraph 19, but the Adjudicator may direct a Party to pay all or part of the fees and expenses. If he makes no such direction, the Parties shall pay them in equal shares. The Party requesting the adjudication shall be liable for the Adjudicator's fees and expenses if the adjudication does not proceed.

30. *Enforcement*

The Parties shall be entitled to the redress set out in the decision and to seek summary enforcement, whether or not the dispute is to be finally determined by legal proceedings or arbitration. No issue decided by the Adjudicator may subsequently be referred for decision by another adjudicator unless so agreed by the Parties.

31. *Subsequent decision by arbitration or court*

In the event that the dispute is referred to legal proceedings or arbitration, the Adjudicator's decision shall not inhibit the right of the court or arbitrator to determine the Parties' rights or obligations as if no adjudication had taken place.

**Miscellaneous Provisions**

32. *Adjudicator not to be appointed arbitrator*

Unless the Parties agree, the Adjudicator shall not be appointed arbitrator in any subsequent arbitration between the Parties under the Contract. No Party may call the Adjudicator as a witness in any legal proceedings or arbitration concerning the subject matter of the adjudication.

33. *Immunity of the Adjudicator*

The Adjudicator is not liable for anything done or omitted in the discharge or purported discharge of his functions as Adjudicator (whether in negligence or otherwise) unless the act or omission is in bad faith, and any employee or agent of the Adjudicator is similarly protected from liability.

34. *Reliance*

The Adjudicator is appointed to determine the dispute or disputes between the Parties and his decision may not be relied upon by third parties, to whom he shall owe no duty of care.

35. Proper law

This procedure shall be interpreted in accordance with the law of England and Wales.

**Definitions**

'Act' means the Housing Grants, Construction and Regeneration Act 1996.

'Adjudicator' means the person named as such in the Contract or appointed in accordance with this Procedure.

'Contract' means the contract between the Parties which contains the provision for adjudication.

'Notice' means the notice given under paragraph 8.

'Party' means a party to the Contract, and any additional parties joined under paragraph 22. 'Referring Party' means the Party who gives notice under paragraph 8.

# AGREEMENT

THIS AGREEMENT is made on the ........................... day of .......................... 19........

Between

1.    ..........................................................

      of ....................................................

      ........................................................(the referring Party)

2.    ..........................................................

      of ....................................................

      ........................................................(the other Party)

(together called the Parties)

3.    ..........................................................

      of ....................................................

      ........................................................(the Adjudicator)

A dispute has arisen between the Parties under a Contract between them dated ...................
in connection with ...........................................................................................................

This dispute has been referred to adjudication in accordance with the CIC Model Adjudication Procedure (the Procedure) and the Adjudicator has been requested to act.

IT IS AGREED that

1.    The rights and obligations of the Adjudicator and the Parties shall be as set out in this Agreement.

2.    The Adjudicator agrees to adjudicate the dispute in accordance with the Procedure.

3.    The Parties agree jointly and severally to pay the Adjudicator's fees and expenses as set out in the attached schedule and in accordance with the Procedure.

4.    The Adjudicator and the Parties shall keep the adjudication confidential, except so far as is necessary to enable a Party to implement or enforce the Adjudicator's decision.

5.    The Parties acknowledge that the Adjudicator shall not be liable for anything done or omitted in the discharge or purported discharge of his functions as Adjudicator (whether in negligence or otherwise) unless the act or omission is in bad faith, and any employee or agent of the Adjudicator shall be similarly protected from liability.

6.    This Agreement shall be interpreted in accordance with the law of England and Wales.

## SCHEDULE

1.    The Adjudicator shall be paid £.......... per hour in respect of all time spent on the adjudication, including travelling time with a maximum of £.......... per day.

2.    The Adjudicator shall be reimbursed his reasonable expenses and disbursements, in respect of travelling, hotel and similar expenses, room charges, the cost of legal or technical advice

obtained in accordance with the Procedure and other extraordinary expenses necessarily incurred.

3.  The Adjudicator is/is not* currently registered for VAT. Where the Adjudicator is registered for VAT, it shall be charged additionally in accordance with the rates current at the date of the work done.

* delete as applicable.

Signed on behalf of the referring Party

...................................................................

Signed on behalf of the other Party

...................................................................

Signed on behalf of the Adjudicator

...................................................................

The MAP and the accompanying Adjudicator Agreement have been drafted by the CIC Adjudication Task Force. A full list of the members of this Task Force is given below. Particular thanks are due to Frances Paterson (Deputy Chairman of the Task Force and Director of Legal Affairs at the Association of Consulting Engineers), Tony Blackler and Phillip Capper.

**Membership of the CIC Adjudication Task Force:**

John Burkett (Chairman), Frances Paterson (Deputy Chairman), John Burgess (Chartered Institute of Building), Neil Burton (Architects & Surveyors Institute), Peter Campbell (Institution of Structural Engineers), Guy Cottam (Institution of Civil Engineers), Chris Dancaster (Royal Institute of Chartered Surveyors), Dennis James (Association of Building Engineers), David Miles (Official Referees Solicitors Association), Keith Rawson (Royal Institute of British Architects), John Riches (Chartered Institute of Building), John Timpson (Royal Institute of British Architects), Brian Totterdill (Institution of Civil Engineers), Bill Weddell (Institution of Civil Engineers), Graham Watts (CIC Chief Executive), Julien Parrott (Secretary, CIC)

# CENTRE FOR DISPUTE RESOLUTION (CEDR) RULES FOR ADJUDICATION INCLUDING GUIDANCE NOTES, APPLICATION FOR APPOINTMENT OF ADJUDICATOR AND CEDR ADJUDICATION AGREEMENT

## PART 1

APPOINTMENT OF ADJUDICATOR & REFERENCE TO ADJUDICATION

A. Where parties to a contract have agreed to refer disputes to adjudication in accordance with these Rules, the following procedure shall apply if the parties are unable to agree on the appointment of an Adjudicator:

(i) Either party may apply to CEDR to appoint the Adjudicator.
(ii) The application shall be made in a form acceptable to CEDR containing brief details of the names and addresses of the parties, a copy of the relevant provisions of the contract providing for adjudication, brief details of the dispute, such other information as may be relevant and a brief statement of the redress sought. CEDR's standard application form is attached to these Rules at Annex A.
(iii) The application shall be accompanied by CEDR's appointment fee due in accordance with CEDR's fee scale at the date of the application by the referring party.
(iv) No later than 7 days after being given notice of an application, CEDR shall (a) appoint the Adjudicator (who shall be provided with a copy of the application) and (b) send the parties the name, address and brief details of the person appointed.

B. The parties will promptly enter into a formal agreement with CEDR and the Adjudicator when requested to do so by CEDR, using CEDR's standard form of agreement which is attached to these Rules at Annex B. Pending signature of an agreement

they shall nonetheless be bound by these Rules as provided in paragraph E below.

C. Where the Adjudicator is named in the contract or is appointed by agreement between the parties without the involvement of CEDR, a party wishing to refer a dispute to the Adjudicator shall give the Adjudicator written notice that a dispute has arisen. The notice shall contain brief details of the names and addresses of the parties, a copy of the relevant provisions of the contract providing for adjudication, brief details of the dispute, such other information as may be relevant and a brief statement of the redress sought. A copy of the notice shall be sent to the other party or parties when it is sent to the Adjudicator. The Adjudicator shall promptly upon receipt of the notice confirm in writing to the parties that the Adjudicator will adjudicate the dispute in accordance with these Rules.

D. Under these Rules the date of referral of the dispute to adjudication shall be:

(i) where paragraph A above applies, the date on which the Adjudicator is appointed by CEDR, or
(ii) where paragraph C above applies, the date on which the parties, under these Rules, are treated as having been given notice of the Adjudicator's confirmation.

E. Parties who have agreed to submit to adjudication in accordance with these Rules shall be bound by these Rules (both Parts 1 & 2).

## PART 2

CONDUCT OF ADJUDICATION PROCEDURE

1. The Adjudicator shall be free to take the initiative in ascertaining the facts and the law and shall have complete discretion as to how to conduct the adjudication. The Adjudicator

shall not be required to observe any rule, whether of evidence or procedure, of any court or tribunal. The Adjudicator shall have complete discretion as to whether or not to hold any meeting with the parties. However, the Adjudicator shall not take into consideration any statement (whether of a party or a witness) unless it has been made available to the parties for consideration.

2. The procedure in paragraph 3 shall apply unless, within 2 days of the date of referral, the Adjudicator either establishes a procedure for the adjudication which does not require the written submissions mentioned below or fixes a preliminary meeting with the parties to be held within 7 days of the date of referral.

3. The party that initiated the reference to adjudication shall, within 4 days of the date of referral, submit to the Adjudicator and to the other party or parties a concise statement of the issues in dispute and the relevant facts. The other party or parties may, not later than 7 days following its receipt, submit a concise statement in response. Either statement may be accompanied by copies of essential documents directly relevant to the dispute.

4. The Adjudicator may at any time request such information and documents from the parties and/or access to any property as the Adjudicator considers appropriate. The parties will respond promptly to any such request.

5. If the Adjudicator at any time wishes to obtain legal or other specialist advice on any matter, he or she shall inform the parties with reasons. However, no adviser shall be appointed by the Adjudicator without the prior consent of both parties.

6. If a party fails to provide any information or documents or to attend any meetings requested by the Adjudicator, then the Adjudicator shall be at liberty to proceed with the adjudication and reach a decision.

7. The Adjudicator shall decide the matters referred to him/her as may in his/her absolute discretion think fit, acting impartially and in good faith. The Adjudicator shall have the power to review and revise any decision made under the terms of the contract to which the dispute relates except where the contract precludes this.

8. The Adjudicator may vary any of the periods specified in these Rules (except for the period for reaching a decision which shall be dealt with as provided in paragraph 9).

## DECISION OF ADJUDICATOR

9. The Adjudicator shall reach a decision as soon as practicable, the objective being to have a decision within 14 days of the date of referral. The Adjudicator may, but shall not be obliged to, give reasons for the decision. The Adjudicator shall in any event reach a decision no later than 28 days from the date of referral. This period may be extended (a) by up to 14 days with the consent of the referring party, or (b) as agreed by the parties. If the Adjudicator requests an extension of the period for the decision but the agreement of the parties is not forthcoming, he or she shall within the time prescribed make such decision as he or she considers appropriate in the circumstances.

10. The parties shall be jointly and severally responsible for the fees and expenses of CEDR and the Adjudicator including the fees and expenses of any adviser appointed under paragraph 5. The Adjudicator shall be entitled to withhold the issue of the decision until payment has been made in full. In the decision, the Adjudicator shall have discretion to apportion liability with regard to the fees and expenses referred to in this paragraph.

11. Every decision of the Adjudicator shall be binding on the parties and notwithstanding paragraphs 12 and 13 shall be implemented without delay by the parties who shall be entitled to such reliefs or remedies as are set out in the decision.

## NOTICE OF DISSATISFACTION

12. If a party is dissatisfied with the decision of the Adjudicator it may, within 60 days of being given notice of the decision (or within such other period as the parties may agree), give written notice of its dissatisfaction to the other party or parties and to the Adjudicator. If no notice of dissatisfaction is issued within this period the decision of the Adjudicator shall be final and binding upon the parties.

13. If a notice of dissatisfaction is given, the dispute will be finally determined by court proceedings or by reference to arbitration in accordance with the contract between the parties. Unless otherwise agreed by the parties, the court or the arbitrator(s) shall not

be bound by, and shall have power to review and revise every decision of the Adjudicator.

## INCAPACITY OF ADJUDICATOR

14. If at any time after the date of referral the Adjudicator becomes unable or unwilling to act, the parties shall endeavour to agree the appointment of a replacement within 7 days of being so notified. If they fail to do so, CEDR shall appoint a replacement Adjudicator within 7 days of receipt of an application from either party and the provisions of Part 1 of these Rules shall be applicable to the new appointment.

## MEDIATION OPTION

15. At any time before the issue of the Adjudicator's decision the parties may agree to refer the dispute to mediation. In that case each party shall notify the Adjudicator and the adjudication shall be suspended. The mediation shall be non-binding until a settlement of the dispute is reached and confirmed in writing by the parties. The Adjudicator shall not act as the mediator. CEDR shall appoint the mediator on the application of either party if the mediator is not agreed between them within 7 days from the date they agree to refer the dispute to mediation. If a settlement of the dispute is not reached within 28 days from the date upon which the parties agree to mediate (or if at any time either party abandons mediation) the adjudication shall recommence. If the dispute is settled by mediation, the adjudication shall be at an end and the parties shall promptly settle the fees and expenses of CEDR and the Adjudicator.

## LIABILITY

16. Neither CEDR nor the Adjudicator shall be liable for anything done or omitted in the discharge of their respective functions unless the act or omission was in bad faith. The same immunity shall extend to any employee or agent of CEDR or of the Adjudicator.

## NOTICES

17. A copy of every notice and document submitted by a party to CEDR or the Adjudicator shall at the same time be sent to the other party/ies. A copy of every document issued by the Adjudicator shall be sent to the parties at the same time. Every notice or document shall be treated as being given 2 working days after it is posted or, in the case of fax or hand delivery, on the day it is delivered (or the next working day if delivery is made after normal working hours).

## MODEL CLAUSE
## FOR APPOINTMENT OF ADJUDICATOR

*Alternative A*

'Any dispute arising under this Agreement may be referred to the Adjudicator by either party. The adjudication shall be conducted in accordance with the CEDR Rules for Adjudication. The Adjudicator's decision shall be in writing and shall promptly be implemented by the parties. An Adjudicator's decision with which a party is dissatisfied shall be resolved by [arbitration/the court] in accordance with this Agreement provided that such party gives notice of dissatisfaction to the other party and to the Adjudicator within the period agreed by the parties or if none within 60 days of the date of the Adjudicator's decision. In the absence of notice, the Adjudicator's decision shall be final and binding on the parties without any right of counterclaim set-off or abatement and, if notice of dissatisfaction is given, the decision shall be binding on and implemented by the parties until the dispute is finally resolved as set out above.

*[The parties agree that notwithstanding the issue of a notice of dissatisfaction, neither of them will serve a notice of arbitration or issue proceedings in relation to a dispute upon which the Adjudicator has issued a decision until after [practical completion] [or earlier termination] of this Agreement.]

If an Adjudicator is not named in this Agreement or if the Adjudicator, having been appointed, becomes unwilling or unable to act at any time, the Adjudicator shall be

---

* Optional extra wording.

appointed by agreement between the parties or in default of agreement by CEDR.'

*Alternative B*

'Any dispute arising under this Agreement which cannot be resolved amicably between the parties shall, in the first instance, be referred to adjudication in accordance with the Rules for Adjudication of CEDR at present in force.'

*Note: Alternative A contains an optional provision which is intended to defer any legal proceedings over the Adjudicator's decision until after 'practical completion'. Both forms can be used whether or not an Adjudicator is named in the contract.*

# CENTRE FOR DISPUTE RESOLUTION

## ANNEX A
## APPLICATION FOR APPOINTMENT OF ADJUDICATOR

To: CEDR

Name and Address of Referring Party:

_____

_____

Date: _____

We, the undersigned, request CEDR to appoint an Adjudicator to deal with certain disputes arising under a contract between us and            of
Brief details of the contract, of the disputes to be adjudicated and of the redress which we seek are set out in the attached Schedule.

A copy of the [Adjudication Agreement/contract clause referring disputes to Adjudication in accordance with CEDR Rules for Adjudication] is attached.

We undertake to indemnify CEDR against any costs or liability which it may incur arising out of this application or any appointment and confirm that we are bound by the CEDR Rules for Adjudication.

We undertake to meet the reasonable fees and expenses of the Adjudicator should the adjudication not proceed for any reason.

We enclose our cheque for £[      ] being the CEDR appointment fee payable in relation to this matter/We are members of CEDR and, therefore, understand that no appointment fee is payable.*

Yours faithfully,

For and on behalf of

(NB: Where a contract provides for adjudication in accordance with CEDR Rules, only one party's signature is necessary. In other cases all parties to the contract should sign an application.)

*(Delete whichever does not apply)

## SCHEDULE

Details of contract and disputes referred to Adjudication:

1. Name and address of each party to the contract.
2. Date of contract.
3. Brief description of subject matter of contract.
4. Brief details of dispute(s) to be referred to adjudication.
5. Brief description of redress being sought.

# CENTRE FOR DISPUTE RESOLUTION
## ANNEX B
## CEDR ADJUDICATION AGREEMENT

DATE ........................................................

PARTIES

1. [      ] of [      ] ('Party A')

2. [      ] of [      ] ('Party B')

3. [      ] of [      ] ('the Adjudicator')

4. Centre For Dispute Resolution Limited trading as Centre for Dispute Resolution (CEDR) of Princes House, 95 Gresham Street, London EC2V 7NA.

**DISPUTE**

(the 'Dispute')

[Here set out details of the contract and brief details of the dispute(s) to be adjudicated.]

1. **Appointment**

   The Adjudicator will adjudicate the Dispute between Party A and Party B (the 'Appointing Parties'). The Adjudicator's appointment shall take effect from [the date of this Agreement].

2. **Conduct of Adjudication**

   The adjudication shall be conducted in accordance with CEDR's Rules for Adjudication a copy of which is annexed and which [as amended in Schedule 1] is incorporated in and forms part of this Agreement.

3. **Costs**

   The Appointing Parties will be jointly and severally responsible to CEDR and the Adjudicator for their respective fees and expenses. Details of the fees and of the initial payment obligations of the Appointing Parties are set out in Schedule 2.

4. **Confidentiality**

   The adjudication and all matters connected with it are and will be kept confidential by the parties except insofar as is necessary to enable a party to implement or enforce the decision of the Adjudicator or for the purpose of any proceedings subsequent to the adjudication.

## 5. Liability

The Appointing Parties expressly acknowledge that neither CEDR nor the Adjudicator (nor any employee or agent of either) shall have any liability for any act or omission, except as provided in CEDR's Rules for Adjudication.

## 6. Law & Jurisdiction

This Agreement shall be governed by English law and under the jurisdiction of the English Courts.

...................................................................

Signed for and on behalf of Party A

...................................................................

Signed for and on behalf of Party B

...................................................................

Signed by the Adjudicator

...................................................................

Signed for and on behalf of CEDR

## SCHEDULE 1

[Here incorporate any amendment to CEDR's Rules for Adjudication agreed between the parties]

## SCHEDULE 2

| | | |
|---|---|---|
| CEDR appointment fee: | £ | |
| Adjudicator's fees: | £ | per day [or part of a day] |
| | £ | per hour |
| Payment to be made on account by each party to CEDR | £ | by [date] |

# CENTRE FOR DISPUTE RESOLUTION

## ADJUDICATION FEES

| | Value of Claim | Adjudication Fee Per Day | Per Party* Per Hour |
|---|---|---|---|
| **1. Adjudication Fees** | Up to £50,000 | £500 | £50 |
| | £50,000–£250,000 | £750 | £75 |
| | £250,000–£500,000 | £1000 | £100 |
| | £500,000–£1m | £1250 | £125 |
| | £1m–£5m | £1500 | £150 |
| | £5m–£10m | £2000 | £200 |
| | £10m upwards | £ Negotiable | |

**2. Adjudication Expenses** such as room hire, Adjudicator's travel expenses, etc.

| **3. Appointment Fee** | **Members of CEDR** | **No Charge** |
|---|---|---|
| | Non-Members | £500 |
| | Clients of Member Firms | £300 |

**4. Alternative Fee Structure in circumstances in which it is difficult to assess the value of the claim will be determined by agreement between CEDR and the parties.**

The fee covers the Adjudicator's fee and the services provided by our ADR Services Unit, which include liaising with/advising all parties in setting up the adjudication, providing preliminary advice, arranging logistical matters with the parties and the Adjudicator, sorting out the terms of the adjudication agreement, dealing with exchange of case summaries and other documentation and identifying and appointing the Adjudicator.

The fee does not include expenses such as room hire, the Adjudicator's travel expenses etc.

If exceptional administrative support is required then there may be an additional fee but only following discussions with the parties.

* Fees for multi-party disputes will be calculated on a 2 party basis plus 25% for each additional party.

## TERMS & CONDITIONS

- The value of the claim will be determined by either the claim or the counterclaim, whichever amount is higher.
- When a claim falls into two fee bands, the higher fee band will apply.

VAT – All the above fees are exclusive of VAT.

## PAYMENT

The Appointment fee (where applicable) is payable by the referring party at the time of referral. Adjudication fees (estimated by CEDR) are payable within 5 working days of issue of invoice.

INVOICING

First Invoice
- Adjudication fees for the number of adjudication days/hours estimated by CEDR (see above for rates); and any known expenses.

Second Invoice
- Any further adjudication fees and expenses not included on the first invoice.
- Full payment of all relevant CEDR invoices prior to issue of the Adjudicator's decision.

ADMINISTRATION

All administrative aspects of the adjudication will be handled by CEDR at no extra cost, unless exceptional administrative support is required.

## ADJUDICATION GUIDANCE NOTES

The numbers and headings in these notes refer to the Rules for Adjudication and accompanying documentation.

Text in square brackets may be inappropriate and therefore inapplicable in some cases.

**The CEDR Adjudication Rules are presently designed for construction adjudications but may also be used for other adjudications.**

### INTRODUCTION

The essence of adjudication is that:

- it involves a neutral third party to decide the matter;
- it is quick, inexpensive and confidential;
- it provides for immediate practical implementation of the results – Rule 11 (subject to possible later confirmation or rectification, if sought – Rule 13);
- the Adjudication Rules are flexible and can be adapted (with or without the assistance of CEDR) to suit the parties.

An adjudication can be used:

- in both domestic and international disputes;
- whether or not litigation or arbitration has been commenced;
- in two party and multi-party disputes.

Rules or rigid procedures in the context of a consensual and adaptable process which is the essence of ADR are generally inappropriate. The Adjudication Rules, the Adjudication Agreement and these Guidance Notes should be sufficient to enable parties to conduct an adjudication.

In some cases the agreement to conduct an adjudication will be as a result of an 'ADR clause' (such as one of the CEDR Model ADR clauses) to that effect in an underlying commercial agreement between the Parties. Where that is the case the Adjudication Rules and the Adjudication Agreement may need to be adapted accordingly.

The Adjudication Agreement, which has been kept as short and simple as possible, incorporates the Adjudication Rules. The Adjudication Agreement can include amendments to the Adjudication Rules; the amendments can be set out in the body of the Adjudication Agreement or the Adjudication Agreement can state the amendments made in the manuscript (or otherwise) to the Adjudication Rules and initialled by the Parties to be incorporated into the Adjudication Agreement.

### CEDR ADJUDICATION PROCEDURE

The procedure is covered under Parts 1 and 2 of the CEDR Rules for Adjudication A to E (Appointment), 1 to 17 (Conduct) with the Model Clause (Appointment) and Application for Appointment (Annex A).

### ADJUDICATION AGREEMENT

If CEDR is asked to do so by a party wishing to initiate an adjudication, it will approach the other party(ies) to a dispute to see if their consent can be obtained.

Ideally the representatives, the advisers (and the Adjudicator if he/she has been identified) and CEDR (or whatever other ADR body is involved, if any) should meet to discuss and finalise the terms of the Adjudication Agreement. Alternatively, the referring party may wish to send a draft agreement based on the CEDR Adjudication Agreement to the other party(ies). The CEDR Adjudication Agreement is set out at Annex B.

### THE ADJUDICATION

The success of the adjudication will, to a large extent, depend on the skill of the Adjudicator. CEDR believes it is very important for the Adjudicator to have had specific training and experience. CEDR has its own body of trained and experienced Adjudicators and can assist the Parties in identifying a suitable Adjudicator.

In some complex cases it may be useful to have more than one Adjudicator, or to have an independent expert who can advise the Adjudicator on technical issues ('the Adjudicator's Adviser'). All should sign the Adjudication Agreement which should be amended as appropriate.

Rules 1 to 17 inclusive cover the actual conduct of the adjudication and the Adjudicator. The decision of the Adjudicator must be implemented immediately notwithstanding any appeal and final revision or review.

## CEDR

The Adjudication Rules envisage the involvement of CEDR because in most cases this is likely to benefit the parties and generally to facilitate the setting up and conduct of the Adjudicator. Its involvement, however, is not essential and the Adjudication Rules can be amended if CEDR is not to be involved.

## DOCUMENTATION

Documentation should be kept as brief as possible and be circulated in accordance with Rule 17.

One of the advantages of adjudication is that it can cut down excessive discovery process (including witness statements) which often blights litigation and arbitration. The documents should be kept to the minimum necessary to give the Adjudicator a good grasp of the issues. The summaries should be similarly brief.

## STAY OF OTHER PROCEEDINGS

Although a stay may engender a better climate for adjudication, it is not however essential that any proceedings relating to the dispute should be stayed. If they are stayed, the effect on limitation periods needs to be agreed.

Although under English law the parties can agree to limitation periods not running, the position may differ in other jurisdictions and the position on this should be checked.

## CONFIDENTIALITY

The CEDR Adjudication Agreement provides that the totality of the adjudication be kept confidential, subject only to later legal proceedings (if any) – Clause 4 of the Adjudication Agreement.

## FEES, EXPENSES AND COSTS

The usual arrangement is for the parties to share equally the fee and expenses of the adjudication, but other arrangements are possible. A party to a dispute which is reluctant to participate in an adjudication may be persuaded to participate if the other party (ies) agree to bear that party's share of the adjudication fees.

## INTERNATIONAL DISPUTES – LANGUAGE AND GOVERNING LAW/ JURISDICTION

The Adjudication Agreement is designed for domestic disputes but can be easily adapted for international cross-border disputes by the addition of the following paragraphs:
'Language
The language of the Adjudicator will be [English]. Any party producing documents or participating in the adjudication in any other language will provide the necessary translations and interpretation facilities.'
'Governing Law and Jurisdiction
The Adjudication Agreement shall be governed by, construed and take effect in accordance with [English] law.
The Courts of [England] shall have exclusive jurisdiction to settle any claim, dispute or matter or difference which may arise out of or in connection with the Adjudicator.'
Where the law is not in English or the jurisdiction not England the Adjudication Agreement may need to be amended to ensure the structure, rights and obligations necessary for an adjudication are applicable.

# FÉDÉRATION INTERNATIONALE DES INGÉNIEURS-CONSEILS (FIDIC) SUPPLEMENT TO FOURTH EDITION 1987 OF CONDITIONS OF CONTRACT FOR WORKS OF CIVIL ENGINEERING CONSTRUCTION: SECTION A – DISPUTE ADJUDICATION BOARD

The following amendments to Clause 67 in Part I General Conditions of the Conditions of Contract for Works of Civil Engineering Construction and to the Appendix to Tender are to be made if it is decided to replace the Engineer as the decision maker by a Dispute Adjudication Board. The amendments to Clause 67 should be included in Part II Conditions of Particular Application.

## AMENDMENTS TO BE MADE TO CLAUSE 67 – SETTLEMENT OF DISPUTES

Delete the text of Clause 67 and substitute:

### Settlement of Disputes and Arbitration

*Dispute Adjudication Board*

**67.1** If a dispute of any kind whatsoever arises between the Employer and the Contractor in connection with, or arising out of, the Contract or the execution of the Works, including any dispute as to any opinion, instruction, determination, certificate or valuation of the Engineer, the dispute shall initially be referred in writing to the Dispute Adjudication Board (the 'Board') for its decision. Such reference shall state that it is made under this Sub-Clause.

Unless the member or members of the Board have been previously mutually agreed upon by the parties and named in the Contract, the parties shall, within 28 days of the Commencement Date, jointly ensure the appointment of the Board. The Board shall comprise suitably qualified persons as members, the number of members being either one or three, as stated in the Appendix to Tender. If the Board is to comprise three members, each party shall nominate one member for the approval of the other party, and the parties shall mutually agree upon and appoint the third member (who shall act as chairman).

The terms of appointment of the Board shall:

(a) incorporate the model terms therefor published by the Fédération Internationale des Ingénieurs-Conseils (FIDIC), as they may have been amended by the parties,

(b) require each member of the Board to be, and to remain throughout his appointment, independent of the parties,

(c) require the Board to act impartially and in accordance with the Contract, and

(d) include undertakings by the parties (to each other and to the Board) that the members of the Board shall in no circumstances be liable for anything done or omitted in the discharge of their functions unless the act or omission is shown to have been in bad faith; the parties shall indemnify the members against such claims.

The terms of the remuneration of each member of the Board, including the remuneration of any expert from whom the Board may seek advice, shall be mutually agreed upon by the Employer, the Contractor and each member of the Board when agreeing the terms of appointment. In the event of disagreement, the remuneration of each member shall include a daily fee in accordance with the daily fee established from time to time for arbitrators under the administrative and financial regulations of the International Centre for Settlement of Investment Disputes, a retainer fee per calendar month equivalent to three times such daily fee and reimbursement for reasonable expenses. The Employer and the Contractor shall each be responsible for paying one-half of the Board's remuneration.

The appointment of any member of the Board may be terminated (other than on a member's own initiative) only by mutual agreement of the Employer and the Contractor. The appointment of each member of the Board shall expire when the discharge referred to in Sub-Clause 60.7 shall have become effective, or at such other time as the parties may mutually agree.

If at any time the parties so agree, they may appoint a suitably qualified person or persons to replace (or to be available to replace) any or all members of the Board. Unless the parties agree otherwise, the appointment will come into effect if a member of the Board declines to act or is unable to act as a result of death, disability, resignation or termination of appointment. If any of such circumstances should occur and no such replacement is available, the member shall be replaced in the same manner as such member was nominated or agreed upon.

If any of the following conditions apply, namely:

- (a) the parties fail to agree upon the appointment of the sole member of a one-person Board within 28 days of the Commencement Date,
- (b) either party fails to nominate a member (acceptable to the other party), for a Board of three members, within 28 days of the Commencement Date,
- (c) the parties fail to agree upon the appointment of the third member (to act as chairman) for a Board of three members within 28 days of the Commencement Date, or
- (d) the parties fail to agree upon the appointment of a replacement member of the Board within 28 days of the date on which a member of the Board declines to act or is unable to act as a result of death, disability, resignation or termination of appointment,

then the appointing body or official named in the Appendix to Tender shall, after due consultation with the parties, appoint such member of the Board, and such appointment shall be final and conclusive.

*Procedure for Obtaining the Board's Decision*

**67.2** When in accordance with Sub-Clause 67.1 a dispute is referred by one party to the Board, a copy of such reference shall be sent by that party to the other party and (for information) to the Engineer. The parties shall promptly make available to the Board all such additional information, further access to the Site, and appropriate facilities, as the Board may require for the purposes of rendering a decision.

The Board shall have full power, among other things, to:

- (a) establish the procedure to be applied in deciding a dispute,
- (b) decide upon the Board's own jurisdiction, and as to the scope of any dispute referred to it,
- (c) take the initiative in ascertaining the facts and matters required for a decision,
- (d) make use of its own specialist knowledge, if any,
- (e) decide upon the payment of interest in accordance with the Contract,
- (f) decide to grant provisional relief such as interim or conservatory measures, and
- (g) open up, review and revise any opinion, instruction, determination, certificate or valuation of the Engineer related to the dispute.

No later than the eighty-fourth day after the day on which it received such reference, the Board, acting as a panel of expert(s) and not as arbitrator(s), shall give notice of its decision, to the parties and (for information) to the Engineer. Such decision, which shall be reasoned, shall state that it is given under this Sub-Clause.

Unless the Contract has already been repudiated or terminated, the Contractor shall, in every case, continue to proceed with the Works with all due diligence, and the Contractor and the Employer, as well as the Engineer, shall give effect forthwith to every decision of the Board, unless and until the same shall be revised, as hereinafter provided, in an amicable settlement or an arbitral award.

If either party is dissatisfied with the Board's decision, then either party, on or before the twenty-eighth day after the day on which it received notice of such decision, may notify the other party and (for information) the Engineer of its dissatisfaction. If the Board fails to give notice of its decision on or before the eighty-fourth day after the day on which it received the reference, then either party, on or before the twenty-eighth day after the day on which the said period of 84 days has expired, may notify the other party and (for information) the Engineer of its dissatisfaction. In either event, such notice of dissatisfaction shall state that it is given under this Sub-Clause, and set out the matter in dispute and the reason(s) for dissatisfaction. Subject to Sub-Clauses 67.5 and 67.6, no arbitration in respect of such dispute may be commenced unless such notice is given.

If the Board has given notice of its decision as to a matter in dispute to the Employer, the Contractor and the Engineer, and no notice of dissatisfaction has been given by either party on or before the twenty-eighth day after the day on which the parties received the Board's decision, then the Board's decision shall become final and binding upon the Employer and the Contractor.

### Amicable Settlement

**67.3** Where notice of dissatisfaction has been given under Sub-Clause 67.2, the parties shall attempt to settle such dispute amicably before the commencement of arbitration. Provided that unless the parties agree otherwise, arbitration may be commenced on or after the fifty-sixth day after the day on which notice of dissatisfaction was given, even if no attempt at amicable settlement has been made.

### Arbitration

**67.4** Any dispute in respect of which:

    (a) the decision, if any, of the Board has not become final and binding pursuant to Sub-Clause 67.2, and
    (b) amicable settlement has not been reached,

shall be settled, unless otherwise specified in the Contract, under the Rules of Conciliation and Arbitration of the International Chamber of Commerce by one or more arbitrators appointed under such Rules. The arbitrator(s) shall have full power to open up, review and revise any decision of the Board, as well as any opinion, instruction, determination, certificate or valuation of the Engineer, related to the dispute.

Neither party shall be limited, in the proceedings before such arbitrator(s), to the evidence or arguments previously put before the Board to obtain its decision.

Arbitration may be commenced prior to or after completion of the Works. Any decision of the Board shall be admissible in evidence in the arbitration. The obligations of the parties, the Engineer and the Board shall not be altered by reason of the arbitration being conducted during the progress of the Works.

### *Failure to Comply with the Board's Decision*

**67.5** Where neither party has given notice of dissatisfaction within the period in Sub-Clause 67.2 and the Board's related decision, if any, has become final and binding, either party may, if the other party fails to comply with such decision, and without prejudice to any other rights it may have, refer the failure itself to arbitration under Sub-Clause 67.4. The provisions of Sub-Clauses 67.2 and 67.3 shall not apply to any such reference.

### *Expiry of the Board's Appointment*

**67.6** When the appointment of the members of the Board, including any replacements, has either been terminated or expired, any such dispute referred to in Sub-Clause 67.2 shall be finally settled by arbitration pursuant to Sub-Clause 67.4. The provisions of Sub-Clauses 67.2 and 67.3 shall not apply to any such reference.

## AMENDMENTS TO BE MADE TO APPENDIX TO TENDER

Add after line which reads

'Rate of interest upon unpaid sums ———— 60.10 ——————— per cent per annum'

the following:

Number of members of
Dispute Adjudication Board (one or three)   67.1   _____

Member of Dispute Adjudication Board (if
not agreed) to be appointed by _____   67.1   The President of FIDIC or a person
                                                   appointed by such President

Number of arbitrators _____   67.4   _____

Place of arbitration _____   67.4   _____

Language(s) of arbitration _____   67.4   _____

If the Rules of Arbitration of the International Chamber of Commerce are not to apply, specify the alternative arbitration rules selected including any additional necessary information. For example, in the case of the UNCITRAL Arbitration Rules, the name of the appointing authority, the number of arbitrators, the place of arbitration and the language(s) to be used in the arbitral proceedings should be specified.

# FIDIC MODEL TERMS OF APPOINTMENT

## TERMS OF APPOINTMENT FOR A BOARD OF THREE MEMBERS[1]

THESE TERMS OF APPOINTMENT OF A BOARD MEMBER ARE MADE BETWEEN:

(1) [*name of Employer*] of [*address of Employer*] (hereinafter called the 'Employer')

(2) [*name of Contractor*] of [*address of Contractor*] (hereinafter called the 'Contractor').

(3) [*name of Board Member*] of [*address of Board Member*] (hereinafter called the 'Board Member')

WHEREAS

A. The Employer and the Contractor (hereinafter jointly referred to as the 'Parties') have on the [ ] day of 199[ ] entered into a Contract (hereinafter called the 'Contract') for the execution of [ ] (hereinafter called the 'Project').

B. By Sub-Clause 67.1 of the Conditions of Contract (hereinafter called the 'Conditions') provision is made for the constitution of a Dispute Adjudication Board (hereinafter called the 'Board') which shall comprise three suitably qualified persons as stated in the Appendix to Tender.

C. The Board Member has agreed to serve as [one of the members of] [chairman of] the Board on the terms set out herein.

NOW IT IS HEREBY AGREED as follows:

1. The Board Member:

   (a) hereby accepts this appointment to the Board which is a personal appointment and agrees to be bound by these Terms of Appointment and Sub-Clauses 67.1 and 67.2 of the Conditions as if they were set out herein; and
   (b) shall be entitled notwithstanding such acceptance to resign this appointment on giving reasonable notice to the Parties.

2. These Terms of Appointment when executed by the Parties and the Board Member shall take effect when the Parties and the last of the three members of the Board have executed terms of appointment.

3. The Board Member shall be and remain impartial and independent of the Parties and shall be under a continuing duty to disclose in writing to each of them and to the other members of the Board any fact or circumstance which might be such as to call into question his impartiality or independence.

   Without prejudice to the generality of the foregoing, the Board Member:

   (a) shall have no interest financial or otherwise in either of the Parties or the Engineer as described in the Contract, or financial interest in the Contract except for payment for services on the Board;
   (b) shall not previously have been employed as a consultant or otherwise by either of the Parties or the Engineer except in those circumstances which have been disclosed in writing to the Parties prior to this appointment;

---

1     Various clauses of these Terms and Rules contain words in brackets [ ], or require that appropriate wording be added. The signatories should consider whether or not these are appropriate in the circumstances of their Project or require amendment.

(c) shall have disclosed in writing to the Parties and to the other members of the Board, prior to this appointment and to his best knowledge and recollection, any professional or personal relationships with any director, officer or employee of the Parties or the Engineer, and any prior involvement in the Project;

(d) shall not while a Board Member be employed as a consultant or otherwise by either of the Parties or the Engineer without the prior written consent of the Parties and the other members of the Board;

(e) shall not give advice to either of the Parties or to the Engineer concerning the conduct of the Project other than in accordance with the Procedural Rules annexed hereto as Appendix A (the 'Rules'); and

(f) shall not while a Board Member enter into discussions or make any agreement with either of the Parties or the Engineer regarding employment by any of them whether as a consultant or otherwise after ceasing to be a Board Member.

4.  The Board Member warrants that he is experienced in the type of work involved in the Project and the interpretation of contract documents and is, as well, fluent in the language of the Contract. The Board Member shall:

(a) ensure his availability for all site visits and hearings as are necessary and shall observe the provisions of the Rules;

(b) become conversant with the Contract and the progress of the Project by studying all documents received which shall be maintained in a current working file;

(c) treat the details of the Contract and all activities and hearings of the Board as private and confidential and shall not publish or disclose the same without the prior written consent of the Parties;

(d) not assign, delegate or subcontract any of the tasks under these Terms of Appointment or the Rules[1];

(e) be available to give advice and opinions in conjunction with other members of the Board on any matter relevant to the Project not being a dispute when requested so to do by the Parties.

5.  Neither the Employer, the Contractor nor the Engineer shall seek advice from or consultation with the Board Member regarding the project otherwise than in the normal course of the Board's activities under the Contract and the Rules. The only exception to this prohibition shall be where the Parties jointly agree to do so and the other Board Members also agree. The Employer shall be responsible for ensuring the compliance by the Engineer with this Clause.

6.  The Board Member will be paid as follows[2]:

(a) a retainer fee of [   ] per calendar month, which shall be considered as payment in full for:

    i. being available on 28 days' notice for all site visits and hearings;

    ii. becoming and remaining conversant with all Project developments and maintaining relevant files;

---

1    Circumstances may arise when the Board considers it needs advice from an outside expert in order to fulfil its duties to the Parties. These Terms do not empower the Board to take such advice at the Parties' expense. It is recommended that in such a situation the Board invite the Parties to agree to secure such advice at their own expense if they accept it is necessary or desirable.

2    It is preferable to agree identical fees for the three Board Members, with the possible exception of the Chairman.

iii. all office and overhead expenses such as secretarial services, photocopying and office supplies incurred in connection with his duties; and

iv. all services performed hereunder except those referred to in Sub-Clauses (b) and (c) below.

Beginning with the month following that in which the Taking-Over Certificate referred to in Sub-Clause 48.1 of the Conditions (or if there is more than one, the one last issued) has been issued, the Board Member shall receive [only one half of the monthly retainer fee]. [Beginning with the next month after expiry of the Defects Liability Period as defined in the Conditions the Board Member shall no longer receive a monthly retainer fee];

(b) a daily fee of [    ] which shall be considered as payment in full for:

i. each day or part of a day up to a maximum of two days travel time in each direction for the journey between the Board Member's home and the site or other location of a Board meeting;

ii. each working day on site visits, hearings or preparing decisions; and

iii. each day spent reading the Parties' submissions in preparation for a hearing;

(c) cost of telephone calls, courier charges, faxes and telexes incurred in connection with his duties; all reasonable and necessary travel expenses including [less than] first class air fare, subsistence and other direct travel expenses. These costs shall be reimbursed in the same currency as that in which fees are payable. Receipts shall be required for all expenses in excess of [    ] percent of the daily fee referred to in Sub-Clause (b) above;

(d) any taxes properly levied in the country of the site on payments made to the Board Member (unless a national or permanent resident of the country of the site) pursuant to this Clause 6. Such reimbursement will be in the same currency as that in which the fees are payable.

The retainer and daily fees shall remain fixed for the [initial] period of tenure of the Board Member [of twelve months]. [Thereafter they shall be adjusted by agreement between the Parties and the Board Member at each anniversary of the execution of these Terms of Appointment].

Payments to the Board Member shall be shared equally by the Employer and the Contractor. The Board Member shall submit invoices for payment of the monthly retainer quarterly in advance. Invoices for daily fees and expenses shall be submitted following the conclusion of a site visit or hearing. All invoices shall be accompanied by a brief description of activities performed during the relevant period and shall be addressed to the Contractor.

The Contractor shall pay Board Members' invoices within 56 calendar days after receipt of such invoices and shall invoice the Employer (through the monthly statements to be submitted in accordance with Sub-Clause 60.1 of the Conditions) for one-half of the amounts of such invoices. The Employer shall pay such Contractor's invoices within the time period specified in the Contract for other payments to the Contractor by the Employer.

Failure of either the Employer or the Contractor to make payment in accordance with these Terms of Appointment shall constitute an event of default under the Contract, entitling the non-defaulting party to take the measures set forth, respectively, in Clause 63 or Clause 69.

Notwithstanding such event of default, and without waiver of rights therefrom, in the event that either the Employer or the Contractor fails to make payment in accordance with these Terms of Appointment, the other party may pay whatever amount may be required to maintain the operation of the Board. The party making such payment, in addition to all other rights arising from such default, shall be entitled to reimbursement of all sums paid in excess of one-half of the amount required to maintain operation of the Board, plus all costs of obtaining such sums and interest thereon.

In the event of non-discharge of Board Members' invoices in accordance with the previous paragraphs the Board Member may either suspend his services until the invoices are discharged or resign his appointment.

7.  The Parties may jointly terminate the Board Member's appointment hereunder by reasonable notice in writing. Such termination shall be without prejudice to any accrued rights of either of the Parties or the Board Member.

8.  The Parties undertake to each other and to the Board Member that the Board Member shall in no circumstances:

    (a) be appointed as an arbitrator in any arbitration between the Parties in connection with the Contract unless the Parties agree otherwise in writing;
    (b) be called as a witness to give evidence concerning any dispute before an arbitrator appointed under the Conditions unless he accepts such assignment in writing addressed to both Parties; or
    (c) be liable for any claims for anything done or omitted in the discharge of such Board Member's functions unless the act or omission is shown to have been in bad faith.

    The Parties hereby jointly and severally indemnify the Board Member against all or any such claims.

9.  If the Board Member shall breach any of the provisions of Clause 3 he shall not be entitled to any fees or expenses hereunder and shall reimburse each of the Employer and the Contractor for any fees and expenses properly paid to him and to any other Board Member if as a consequence of such breach any proceedings or decisions of the Board are rendered void or ineffective.

10. These Terms of Appointment shall be governed by the law of [    ].

11. Any dispute or claim arising out of or in connection with these Terms of Appointment or the breach, termination or invalidity thereof, shall be finally settled under the Rules of Conciliation and Arbitration of the International Chamber of Commerce by a sole arbitrator appointed in accordance with said Rules.

| SIGNED by _____ for and on behalf of the Employer in the presence of | SIGNED by _____ for and on behalf of the Contractor in the presence of | SIGNED by the Board Member in the presence of |
|---|---|---|
| Witness: | Witness: | Witness: |
| Name: | Name: | Name: |
| Address: | Address: | Address: |
| Date: | Date: | Date: |

# FIDIC PROCEDURAL RULES

## APPENDIX A: PROCEDURAL RULES OF THE DISPUTE ADJUDICATION BOARD (OF THREE MEMBERS)

1. The Board shall visit the site at regular intervals [and/or at times of critical construction events] at the request of either the Employer or the Contractor, and in any event not less than [three] times in any twelve month period.

2. The timing of and agenda for each site visit shall be as agreed jointly by the Board, the Employer and the Contractor, or in the absence of agreement, shall be decided by the Board.

3. The purpose of site visits is to enable the Board to become and remain acquainted with the progress of the Project and of any actual or potential problems or claims.

   Site visits shall be attended by the Employer, the Contractor and the Engineer and shall be co-ordinated by the Employer in co-operation with the Contractor. The Employer shall ensure the provision of appropriate conference facilities and secretarial and copying services.

   At the conclusion of each site visit and before leaving the site the Board shall prepare a report on its activities during the visit and shall send copies to those parties who attended.

4. The Employer and the Contractor shall furnish to each Board Member one copy of all documents which the Board may request, including Contract documents, progress reports, variation instructions, certificates and other documents pertinent to the performance of the Contract.

5. If any dispute is referred to the Board in accordance with Sub-Clause 67.2 of the Conditions, the Board shall proceed as described therein. The Board may in its discretion, among other things, conduct a hearing on the dispute in which event it will decide on the date and place for the hearing and may request that written documentation and arguments from the Employer and the Contractor be presented to it prior to or at the hearing. Subject to the time imparted to the Board to give notice of a decision and other relevant factors, the Board shall afford to each of the Employer and the Contractor reasonable opportunity to present its case in relation to a dispute referred to the Board for decision.

   The Board shall act as a Board of impartial experts, not arbitrators, and shall have full authority to conduct any hearing as it thinks fit, not being bound by any rules or procedures other than those set out herein. [Without limiting the foregoing, the Board shall have power to adopt an inquisitorial procedure, to refuse admission to hearings or audience at hearings to any persons other than the Employer, the Contractor and the Engineer and to proceed in the absence of any party who the Board is satisfied received notice of the hearing.]

   The Board shall not express any opinions during any hearing concerning the merits of any arguments advanced by the Parties. After a hearing is concluded the Board shall convene in private to formulate its decision.

   [If a member fails to attend a meeting or hearing, or to fulfil any required function, the other two members may nevertheless proceed and make decisions unless the absent member is the chairman and instructs the other two members not to proceed, or the Parties otherwise agree.]

6. The Board shall give notice of its decision in writing to the Employer and the Contractor in accordance with Sub-Clause 67.2 of the Conditions or as otherwise agreed by the Employer and the Contractor in writing.

   The Board shall endeavour to reach decisions unanimously, but if this is impossible decisions shall be by a majority and the minority member may prepare a written report for submission to the Employer, the Engineer and the Contractor.

7. All communications between either of the Parties and a Board Member and all hearings shall be in the [    ] language. All such communications shall be copied to the other Party and to other members of the Board.

*Source:* Fédération Internationale des Ingénieurs-Conseils (FIDIC). This section is subject to copyright and may not be reproduced without the written permission of FIDIC; copies may be obtained from the FIDIC bookshop: FIDIC Secretariat, PO Box 86, 1000 Lausanne 12, Switzerland.

# Appendix 4

## LIST OF NOMINATING BODIES

### NOMINATING BODY FOR ADJUDICATORS

| | |
|---|---|
| **Body:** | Academy of Construction Adjudicators (ACA) |
| **Contact:** | Mr Milne |
| **Telephone no:** | 0421 409 292 |
| **Fax no:** | 01684 567 080 |
| **Address:** | Parabola House, Parabola Road, Cheltenham, Gloucestershire GL50 3AH |
| **Appointment fee:** | £150 |

| | |
|---|---|
| **Body:** | Centre for Dispute Resolution (CEDR) |
| **Contact:** | Andy Grossman/ADR Services Unit |
| **Telephone no:** | 0171 600 0500 |
| **Fax no:** | 0171 600 0501 |
| **Address:** | Princes House, 95 Gresham Street, London EC2V 7NA |
| **Appointment fee:** | Free to members. £300 to clients of firms (such as solicitors claim consultants) who are members. £500 to non-members. |

| | |
|---|---|
| **Body:** | Chartered Institute of Arbitrators (CIArb) |
| **Contact:** | Gillian Michelotti |
| **Telephone no:** | 0171 837 4483 |
| **Fax no:** | 0171 837 4185 |
| **Address:** | 24 Angel Gate, City Road, London EC1V 2FB |
| **Appointment fee:** | £225 + VAT |

| | |
|---|---|
| **Body:** | Chartered Institute of Builders (CIOB) |
| **Contact:** | Julie Rimmel |
| **Telephone no:** | 01344 630 700 |
| **Fax no:** | 01344 630 777 |
| **Address:** | Englemere, Kings Ride, Ascot, Berks SL5 7TB |
| **Appointment fee:** | £150 |

| | |
|---|---|
| **Body:** | Confederation of Construction Specialists (CCS) |
| **Contact:** | John Huxtable |
| **Telephone no:** | 01252 312 122 |
| **Fax no:** | 01252 343 081 |
| **Address:** | 75/79 High Street, Aldershot, Hampshire SU11 1BX |
| **Appointment fee:** | £50 + VAT for members. £100 + VAT for non-members. |

| | |
|---|---|
| **Body:** | Construction Federation |
| **Contact:** | Margaret Rowlands/Jocelyn Duigan |
| **Telephone no:** | 0171 608 5000 |

**Fax no:**              0171 608 5041
**Address:**             Construction House, 56–64 Leonard Street, London EC2A 4JX
**Appointment fee:**     £100 + VAT

**Body:**                Construction Industry Council (CIC)
**Contact:**             Julien Farcott/John Mead
**Telephone no:**        0171 637 8692
**Fax no:**              0171 580 6140
**Address:**             26 Stone Street, London WC1E 7BT
**Appointment fee:**     £150 + VAT

**Body:**                Institution of Chemical Engineers
**Contact:**             Derry Rolfe
**Telephone no:**        01788 578 214
**Fax no:**              01788 560 833
**Address:**             Davis Building, 165–179 Railway Terrace, Rugby CV21 3HQ
**Appointment fee:**     £200 + VAT

**Body:**                Institute of Electrical Engineers (IEE)
**Contact:**             Brian Lewis
**Telephone no:**        0171 240 1871
**Fax no:**              0171 497 2143
**Address:**             Savoy Place, London WC2R 0BI
**Appointment fee:**     £100 + VAT

**Body:**                Institution of Civil Engineers (ICE)
**Contact:**             Eithne Stanton
**Telephone no:**        0171 665 2215
**Fax no:**              0171 222 1403
**Address:**             1 Great George Street, Westminster, London SW1P 3AA
**Appointment fee:**     £176 (inclusive of VAT)

**Body:**                The Technology and Construction Court Bar Association (TECBAR)
**Contact:**             Caroline McCombe/Simon Slattery
**Telephone no:**        0171 353 2656
**Fax no:**              0171 383 2036
**Address:**             4 Pump Court, London EC4Y 7AN
**Appointment fee:**     Free

**Body:**                The Technology and Construction Court Solicitors Association
                         (TeCSA)
**Contact:**             Robert Fenwick Elliott
**Telephone no:**        0171 956 9354
**Fax no:**              0171 956 9355/64
**e-mail:**              RJFE@fenwickelliot.co.uk
**Appointment fee:**     £100 + VAT

**Body:**                Royal Institute of British Architects (RIBA)
**Contact:**             Keith Snook/J Brown
**Telephone no:**        0171 307 3679 / 0171 307 3649
**Fax no:**              0171 307 3754

**Address:**      66 Portland Street, London W1N 4AD
**Appointment fee:**  £150 + VAT

**Body:**      Royal Institute of Chartered Surveyors (RICS)
**Contact:**    Martin Burns/Carol Goodall
**Telephone no:**  0171 334 3808
**Fax no:**  0171 334 3802
**Address:**  The RICS Dispute Resolution Service, Surveyor Court, Westwood Way, Coventry CV4 8JE
**Appointment fee:**  £200 + VAT

**Body:**    3A Adjudicators
**Contact:**  Rod Badenhelard
**Telephone no:**  0181 293 9533
**Fax no:**  0181 293 9633
**Address:**  Meridian House, 148A Greenwich High Road, London SE10 8NN
**Appointment fee:**  £50 for post-dispute appointment.

# Index

References are to paragraph numbers; *italic* page numbers are to Appendix material.